W9-CCO-845

THIS GUIDE BELONGS TO:

_____

_____

_____

Resources from Bruce Bugbee

Network (with Don Cousins)
What You Do Best in the Body of Christ
Discover Your Spiritual Gifts the Network Way

A NETWORK MINISTRY RESOURCE

network

PARTICIPANT'S GUIDE revised

he right people, in the right places, for the right reasons, at the right time

bruce bugbee and don cousins

with wendy seidman

ZONDERVAN™

GRAND RAPIDS, MICHIGAN 49530 USA

WILLOW

Willow Creek Resources

ZONDERVAN™

Network Participant's Guide — Revised
Copyright © 1994, 2005 by Willow Creek Community Church and Bruce Bugbee

Requests for information should be addressed to:
Zondervan, *Grand Rapids, Michigan 49530*

ISBN-10: 0-310-25795-6
ISBN-13: 978-0-310-25795-0

Printed in the United States of America

06 07 08 09 10 11 /❖ DCI/ 10 9 8 7 6 5 4 3

To My Four Children:
Brittany, Brianne, Bronwyn, and Todd
and
to their children's children

Contents

Appendix

Foreword

God's thumbprint is on each of us from the time we are born. Through the power of your own personal story, the revised edition of Network takes you on a wonderful journey that assists you in discovering your spiritual gifts, your style, and your passion. Network is a holistic discovery process that assists every believer in finding their unique contribution in ministry.

A Gold Medallion Award winner, Network—created by Bruce Bugbee, Don Cousins, and Bill Hybels of Willow Creek Community Church—has helped over a million people discover their gifts.

Bruce Bugbee has faithfully responded to God's call on his life by teaching gift-based ministry for the last eighteen years. Network reflects his desire to serve and grow God's people, as well as make these outstanding, user-friendly tools accessible to all who desire to teach them.

I urge you to journey down this path of discovery. I can testify to the fact that learning and claiming your unique identity in Christ through Network is transformational.

Sue Mallory
Executive Director of Leadership Connection
Author of *The Equipping Church*

Acknowledgments

This is the third edition of Network. With each major revision the circle of contributors to the Network process expands. Therefore Network continues to develop and impact the lives of those who are seeking to serve according to who God has created and called to serve.

The Willow Creek Association and Zondervan are committed to building biblical functioning communities through prevailing churches who are equipping God's people to serve with their spiritual gifts. Their vision is at the foundation of this latest edition of Network. Together we continue to serve the prevailing church.

I'd like to thank Bill Hybels, senior pastor of Willow Creek Community Church, for his integral role in creating the Network resource in its original form. He has always been a champion for the value that every church should be a unified community of servants stewarding their spiritual gifts.

I again had the privilege to work with Wendy Seidman to rethink and reshape this latest edition of Network. Our experience is a testimony to the words, "iron sharpens iron" (Proverbs 27:17). God has forged a sharper tool for the kingdom to encourage and support prevailing churches.

Bette Holderman has provided much encouragement and office support to bring this project together. She has been a longtime staff member and served the people, pastors, and churches around the world with grace.

It was a joy to serve with Nancy Raney, who provided the project management needed to keep us on task and coordinate the many facets of this project.

I am grateful for my wife, Wendy, for the support she has given me throughout the many months of this writing. Her sacrifices and support have served me, you, and the church.

And now to the greatest contributor of all, Jesus Christ—the head of the church, I give thanks for calling me to such a ministry as this. I am a blessed man to be able to serve those who are seeking to serve and equip the leaders equipping them.

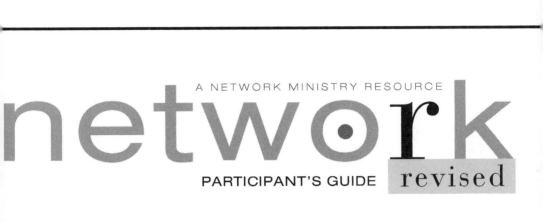

A NETWORK MINISTRY RESOURCE

network

PARTICIPANT'S GUIDE · revised

Introduction

The church needs you. Not because it needs people to fill positions within the organization, but because YOU are an important and integral part of the body of Christ. You have a significant contribution to make. You have a ministry in the church and a mission in the world.

My personal journey with Spiritual Gifts began in 1969. Through the years, there have been many mentors, experiences and opportunities to grow and develop. I am still learning. My calling has also given me opportunities to lead and mentor others.

Since the formation of Network in 1986, over one million people have found a renewed energy for the local church and personal ministry. Network is used in local and international churches with resources in twelve languages.

I am called and committed to support local churches that are seeking to be prevailing churches. Healthy churches are functioning on the basis of gift-based ministry teams. They have systems in place for personal discovery and ministry connection. They are intentional and they are individual.

While there has been overwhelming affirmation for the Network process through the years, it seemed time to make some adjustments. This revision of Network applies some of our latest findings and offers them in a more effective format with new and updated DVDs.

So, welcome to these revised Network materials. Network will help increase your spiritual power in and through the local church!

Doing gift-based ministry is not optional. It is biblical. It is God's *operating system* for his church. Envision the goal. Enjoy the process and be equipped. Diligently serve as you have been created and called to do, and you will glorify God and edify others!

Bruce Bugbee
Network Ministries International
Ladera Ranch, California
www.networkministries.com

"Imagine a Church ..."

My Father is glorified by this, that you bear much fruit.

John 15:8 NASB

These things I have spoken to you so that My joy may be in you, and that your joy may be made full.

John 15:11NASB

GROUPS: IMAGINE A CHURCH . . .

Directions

1. Get into groups of three.

2. Introduce yourself to the group.

3. Discuss the observations and insights you had from the DVD.

NETWORK'S GOAL

Network's Goal is to help believers to be fruitful and fulfilled in a meaningful place of service.

> *You, my brothers, were called to be free. But do not use your freedom to indulge the sinful nature; rather, **serve one another in love.***
>
> Galatians 5:13

Serving is not optional, it is a matter of

OBEDIENCE.

Network will help you better understand

- Who God has made you to be
- When you make your unique contribution, you make a kingdom difference for eternity

Network takes the pieces you already have and puts them in a framework that helps you see the picture God intended for your life.

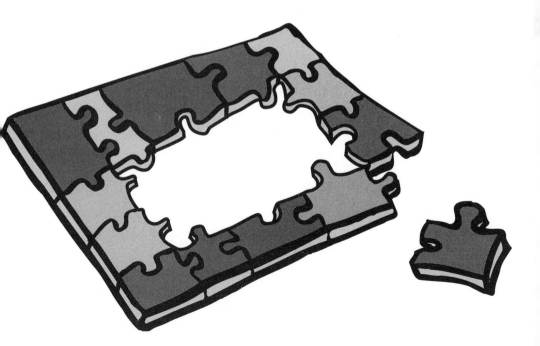

THE NETWORK PROCESS

Step One: *Discovery*

You will learn more about your God-given *Servant Profile*.

Step Two: *Coaching*

A Coach will assist you in finding a meaningful place of service according to your *Servant Profile*.

Step Three: SERVICE

The goal is meaningful service.

WHY DO WE SERVE ANYWAY?

There is a twofold biblical purpose for serving. We are to

- Glorify God
- Edify Others

There are two key passages:

1. The Ten Commandments (Exodus 20:1–17)

   1. Don't have other gods

   2. Don't worship idols

   3. Don't take God's name in vain

   4. Remember the Sabbath

The focus of these four is "___GOD___" and how we are to love him.

   5. Honor parents

   6. Don't murder

   7. Don't commit adultery

   8. Don't steal

   9. Don't be a false witness

   10. Don't covet

The focus of these six is "___OTHERS___" and how we are to love them.

2. The Great Commandment (Matthew 22:37–40)

"Love the Lord your God with all your heart and with all your soul and with all your mind." This is the first and greatest commandment. And the second is like it: "Love your neighbor as yourself." All the Law and the Prophets hang on these two commandments.

In these Old and New Testament passages we see the Bible's twofold emphasis. We are to

- Love or glorify God

- Love or edify others

Our serving glorifies God because it is a form of worship.

*Therefore, I urge you, brothers, in view of God's mercy, to offer your bodies as living sacrifices, holy and pleasing to God—this is your **spiritual act of worship.***

Romans 12:1

*Whoever speaks, is to do so as one who is speaking the utterances of God; **whoever serves is to do so as one who is serving by the strength which God supplies; so that in all things God may be glorified** through Jesus Christ, to whom belongs the glory and dominion forever and ever. Amen.*

1 Peter 4:11 NASB

Our serving builds up or edifies others.

> *It was he who gave some to be apostles, some to be prophets, some to be evangelists, and some to be pastors and teachers, to prepare [equip] God's people for works of service, **so that the body of Christ may be built up** [edified].*
>
> Ephesians 4:11–12

THE MAJOR TEST OF SERVICE

When we serve, does it glorify God and edify others?

HOW WE'RE TO SERVE

THE *SERVANT PROFILE*		
SPIRITUAL GIFTS indicate:	**WHAT** you do best	You will be **COMPETENT!**
PERSONAL STYLE indicates:	**HOW** you best serve	You will be **CONFIDENT!**
MINISTRY PASSION indicates:	**WHERE** you best serve	You will be **MOTIVATED!**

There are . . .

> no right or wrong gifts
>
>> no right or wrong styles
>>
>>> no right or wrong passions
>>>
>>>> . . . they are just different!

You can have . . .

> any Spiritual Gift, with
>
>> any Personal Style, with
>>
>>> any Ministry Passion!

SERVANT PROFILE: SPIRITUAL GIFTS

There are three truths about all Spiritual Gifts:

1. Spiritual Gifts are God-given.

2. There are no right or wrong Spiritual Gifts. They are just different.

3. Spiritual Gifts answer the "__WHAT__" question: What should I do when I serve?

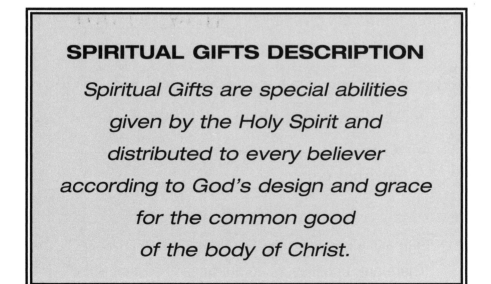

SPIRITUAL GIFTS DESCRIPTION

Spiritual Gifts are special abilities given by the Holy Spirit and distributed to every believer according to God's design and grace for the common good of the body of Christ.

Spiritual Gifts are special abilities.

- They are divine endowments.

- They are used for spiritual purposes.

- They are tasks or functions.

- They enable us to do meaningful service.

> *To one there is given through the Spirit the message of wisdom, to another the message of knowledge by means of the same Spirit, to another faith by the same Spirit, to another gifts of healing by that one Spirit, to another miraculous powers, to another prophecy . . .*
>
> 1 Corinthians 12:8–10

Spiritual Gifts are given by the HOLY SPIRIT.

- God gives these gifts to his children.

- Every believer has at least one Spiritual Gift.

- We do not earn them or choose them.

- Without the Holy Spirit, there are no Spiritual Gifts.

God gives these gifts to his children—to believers. Therefore, unbelievers do not have "Spiritual Gifts."

Spiritual Gifts are distributed to every believer according to God's design and grace.

- They show us how we can make our unique contribution.

- They reveal a part of God's will for our lives.

- They confirm that every believer has a place of service.

- They are given for power and purpose in our ministry.

Each one should use whatever gift he has received **to serve others,** *faithfully administering God's grace in its various forms.*

1 Peter 4:10

Now to each one the manifestation of the Spirit is given **for the common good.**

1 Corinthians 12:7

Spiritual Gifts are for the <u>COMMON GOOD</u> *of the body of Christ.*

- My gifts aren't for me, they are to benefit others.

- They are given to build up other believers.

- They help us to serve one another better.

- They empower believers to expand the kingdom of God.

Your Spiritual Gift is not *for* you. It is given *to* you *for* others!

God carefully selected each believer's Spiritual Gift(s).

*Now to **each one** the manifestation of the Spirit is given for the common good.*

1 Corinthians 12:7

*All these are the work of one and the same Spirit, and He gives them to **each one, just as he determines.***

1 Corinthians 12:11

*But in fact God has arranged the parts in the body, **every one of them, just as he wanted them to be.***

1 Corinthians 12:18

Reflection:

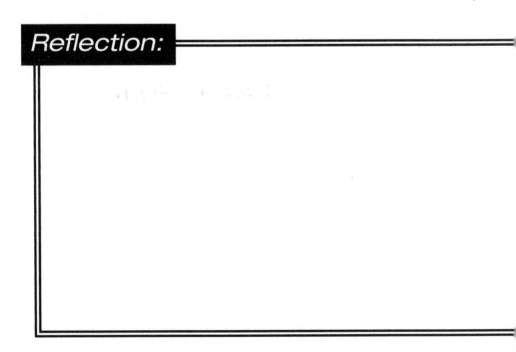

UNIQUENESS, UNITY, AND DIVERSITY

Our Spiritual Gifts are given by design and make us unique.

> *We have different gifts, according to the grace given us.*
>
> Romans 12:6

Diversity is not ___DIVISION___.

> *As it is, there are many parts, but one body. The eye cannot say to the hand, "I don't need you!" And the head cannot say to the feet, "I don't need you!" . . . so that there should be no division in the body, but that its parts should have equal concern for each other. If one part suffers, every part suffers with it; if one part is honored, every part rejoices with it.*
>
> 1 Corinthians 12:20–21, 25–26

The diversity of these spiritual manifestations is simply a reflection of who God is.

> *There are different kinds of gifts, but the same Spirit. There are different kinds of service, but the same Lord. There are different kinds of working, but the same God works all of them in all {people}.*
>
> 1 Corinthians 12:4–6

Just as diversity was not meant to be division, so unity is not conformity.

> *Are all apostles? Are all prophets? Are all teachers? Do all work miracles? Do all have gifts of healing? Do all speak in tongues? Do all interpret?*
>
> 1 Corinthians 12:29–30

> *If the whole body were an eye, where would the sense of hearing be? If the whole body were an ear, where would the sense of smell be? But in fact God has arranged the parts in the body, every one of them, just as he wanted them to be. If they were all one part, where would the body be? As it is, there are many parts, but one body.*
>
> 1 Corinthians 12:17–20

Unity is not achieved by being alike.

Unity is achieved by having the same <u>PURPOSE</u> to glorify God and to edify others.

INTERDEPENDENCE

SUMMARY

- Network's Goal is to help believers to be fruitful and fulfilled in a meaningful place of service.

- We serve to glorify God and to edify others.

- We are to serve according to our *Servant Profile*.

- The *Servant Profile* identifies our

    Spiritual Gifts, which answers the "What" question

    Personal Style, which answers the "How" question

    Ministry Passion, which answers the "Where" question

- Spiritual Gifts are special abilities given by the Holy Spirit and distributed to every believer according to God's design and grace for the common good of the body of Christ.

RECOMMENDATION: Participants will benefit from reading Bruce Bugbee's *What You Do Best in the Body of Christ* along with these Discovery Sessions. The book includes additional insights, questions, and suggestions for personal reflection.

"The Purpose of Gifts"

In Christ we who are many form one body, and each member belongs to all the others.

Romans 12:5

But to each one is given the manifestation of the Spirit for the common good.

1 Corinthians 12:7 NASB

DEPENDENCE / INDEPENDENCE / INTERDEPENDENCE

We all start out in *dependent* relationships.

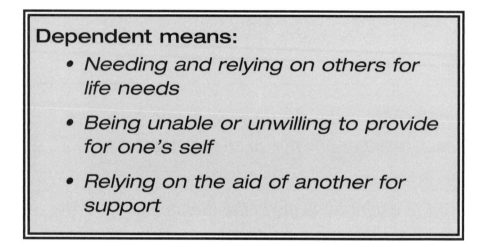

Dependent means:

- *Needing and relying on others for life needs*

- *Being unable or unwilling to provide for one's self*

- *Relying on the aid of another for support*

Some become *independent*.

Culturally, we equate ___MATURITY___
with independence.

Independent means:

- *Not needing or relying on others for life or relational needs*

- *Being able to provide for one's self*

- *Free from the influence, guidance, and control of others*

God calls us to be *interdependent* and have interdependent relationships.

Interdependent means:

- *Committing who we are and what we have to serve others*

- *Knowing what we can offer to, and what we need from, others*

- *Enjoying the fruit of diverse gifts operating in unison ("mutually dependent")*

Interdependent relationships reflect God's design for the church.

In Christ we who are many form one body, and each member belongs to all the others.

Romans 12:5

Now you are the body of Christ, and each one of you is a part of it.

1 Corinthians 12:27

When we all do what we were created to do . . .

and we do it together . . .

we will be a healthy, interdependent, and harmonious church.

GROUPS: INCREASING OUR INTERDEPENDENCE

Directions

1. Get into groups of three.

2. Share with your group what keeps you, personally, from being more interdependent.

3. Identify one step you could take to become more interdependent.

4. Write your answer in the space provided.

What keeps me from being more interdependent:

_____

Step(s) I will take to become more interdependent:

_____

A LIST OF SPIRITUAL GIFTS

Directions

We will do this together.

1. Read each passage of Scripture and as a Spiritual Gift is identified, write that Gift in the space provided.

2. A few of the Spiritual Gifts are mentioned more than once. We will only write down a gift the first time we see it, because we are simply trying to come up with a list of them.

SCRIPTURE PASSAGE	GIFTS MENTIONED
1 Corinthians 12:8–10 (NASB) *For to one is given the **word of wisdom** through the Spirit, and to another the **word of knowledge** according to the same Spirit; to another **faith** by the same Spirit, and to another gifts of **healing** by the one Spirit, and to another the effecting of **miracles,** and to another **prophecy,** and to another the distinguishing of spirits **[discernment],** to another various kinds of **tongues,** and to another the **interpretation** of tongues.*	1. _____ 2. _____ 3. _____ 4. _____ 5. _____ 6. _____ 7. _____ 8. _____ 9. _____

SCRIPTURE PASSAGE	GIFTS MENTIONED
1 Corinthians 12:28 (NASB) *And God has appointed in the church, first apostles **[apostleship]**, second prophets, third teachers **[teaching]**, then miracles, then gifts of healings, **helps, administrations,** various kinds of tongues.*	10. _____ 11. _____ 12. _____ 13. _____
Romans 12:6–8 (NASB) *Since we have gifts that differ according to the grace given to us, each of us is to exercise them accordingly: if prophecy, according to the proportion of his faith; if service, in his serving; or he who teaches, in his teaching; or he who exhorts, in his exhortation **[encouragement]**; he who gives **[giving]**, with liberality; he who leads **[leadership]**, with diligence; he who shows **mercy,** with cheerfulness.*	14. _____ 15. _____ 16. _____ 17. _____
Ephesians 4:11 (NASB) *And He gave some as apostles, and some as prophets, and some as evangelists **[evangelism]**, and some as pastors **[shepherding]** and teachers.*	18. _____ 19. _____

NOTE: In these four passages, you can clearly see some of the Spiritual Gifts. But these lists are not identical . . . they vary in order and content. These lists are used more as illustrative *examples* of the Spiritual Gifts than as a *definitive* list of Gifts. Spiritual Gifts are

- Rooted in Scripture
- Clearly evident in the life of the local church
- Affirmed in the lives of some believers
- Consistent with our description of a Spiritual Gift

SCRIPTURE PASSAGE	GIFTS MENTIONED
1 Peter 4:9–10 *Offer **hospitality** to one another without grumbling. Each one should use whatever gift he has received to serve others, faithfully administering God's grace in its various forms.*	20. _____
Exodus 31:3–5 (NASB) *I have filled him with the Spirit of God in wisdom, in understanding, in knowledge, and in all kinds of craftmanship to make artistic designs for work in gold, in silver, and in bronze, and in the cutting of stones for settings, and in the carving of wood, that he may work in all kinds of **craftsmanship.***	21. _____
1 Timothy 2:1–2 *I urge, then, first of all, that requests, prayers, **intercession** and thanksgiving be made for everyone—for kings and all those in authority, that we may live peaceful and quiet lives in all godliness and holiness.*	22. _____
Psalm 150:3–5 (NASB) *Praise Him with trumpet sound; Praise Him with harp and lyre. Praise Him with timbrel and dancing; Praise Him with stringed instruments and pipe. Praise Him with loud cymbals; Praise Him with resounding cymbals **[creative communication]**.*	23. _____

Some churches recognize other possible gifts not described or mentioned in Network, such as celibacy, counseling, deliverance, martyrdom, and voluntary poverty.

> *A guiding principle to determine what a Spiritual Gift is, is to look at the life and ministry of Jesus Christ.*

GROUPS: MATCHING

Directions

1. Get back into your groups.

2. One person read a description aloud as the others read along silently.

3. Match each Spiritual Gift with its description.

4. Write the letter of the description in the blank below the Spiritual Gift. For example, after reading description *A*, you see that *apostleship* matches *A*.

5. The six descriptions in Group 1 correspond to the six Spiritual Gifts listed in Group 1. This is also true for Groups 2, 3, and 4.

6. You will complete the "Contributes" column later.

7. The purpose of this exercise is for you to become familiar with all the Spiritual Gifts and their descriptions, not just your own.

This is not a race, so read through each description completely before matching it with the Spiritual Gift.

GROUP 1: *Spiritual Gifts Matching*

	1	2	3
SPIRITUAL GIFT	ADMINISTRATION	APOSTLESHIP	CRAFTSMANSHIP
MATCHES		A	
CONTRIBUTES			

A. The divine enablement to start and oversee the development of new churches or ministry structures. People with this gift: pioneer and establish new ministries in churches, adapt to different surroundings by being culturally sensitive and aware, desire to minister to unreached people in other communities or countries, have responsibilities to oversee ministries or groups of churches, demonstrate authority and vision for the mission of the church.

B. The divine enablement to understand what makes an organization function and the special ability to plan and execute procedures that accomplish ministry goals. People with this gift: develop strategies or plans to reach identified goals, assist ministries to become more effective and efficient, create order out of organizational chaos, manage or coordinate a variety of responsibilities to accomplish a task or event.

C. The divine enablement to distinguish between truth and error, discern the spirits, differentiating between good and evil, right and wrong. People with this gift: distinguish truth from error, right from wrong, pure motives from impure, identify deception in others with accuracy and appropriateness, determine whether a word attributed to God is authentic, recognize inconsistencies in a teaching, prophetic message, or interpretation, are able to sense the presence of evil.

GROUP 1: *Spiritual Gifts Matching*

	4	5	6
SPIRITUAL GIFT	**CREATIVE COMMUNICATION**	**DISCERNMENT**	**ENCOURAGEMENT**
MATCHES			
CONTRIBUTES			

D. The divine enablement to creatively design and/or construct items to be used for ministry. People with this gift: work with wood, cloth, paints, metal, glass, and other raw materials, make things that increase the effectiveness of others' ministries, enjoy serving with their hands to meet tangible needs, design and build tangible items and resources for ministry use, work with different kinds of tools and are skilled with their hands.

E. The divine enablement to present truth so as to strengthen, comfort, or urge to action those who are discouraged or wavering in their faith. People with this gift: strengthen and reassure those who are discouraged, challenge, comfort, or confront others to trust and hope in the promises of God, urge others to action by applying biblical truth, motivate others to grow, emphasize God's promises, and have confidence in his will.

F. The divine enablement to communicate God's truth through a variety of art forms. People with this gift: use the arts to communicate God's truth, develop and use artistic skills such as drama, writing, art, music, dance, etc., use variety and creativity to captivate people and cause them to consider Christ's message, challenge people's perspectives of God through various forms of the arts, demonstrate fresh ways to express the Lord's ministry and message.

GROUP 2: *Spiritual Gifts Matching*

	7	8	9
SPIRITUAL GIFT	EVANGELISM	FAITH	GIVING
MATCHES			
CONTRIBUTES			

G. The divine enablement to accomplish practical and necessary tasks that free up, support, and meet the needs of others. People with this gift: serve behind the scenes wherever needed to support the gifts and ministries of others, see the tangible and practical things to be done and enjoy doing them, sense God's purpose and pleasure in meeting everyday responsibilities, attach spiritual value to practical service, enjoy knowing that they are making it possible for others to do what God has called them to do.

H. The divine enablement to care for people by providing fellowship, food, and shelter. People with this gift: provide an environment in which people feel valued and cared for, meet new people and help them feel welcomed, create a safe and comfortable setting where relationships can develop, seek ways to connect people together into meaningful relationships, set people at ease in unfamiliar surroundings.

I. The divine enablement to act on God's promises with confidence and unwavering belief in his ability to fulfill his purposes. People with this gift: believe the promises of God and inspire others to do the same, act in complete confidence of God's ability to overcome obstacles, demonstrate an attitude of trust in God's will and his promises, advance the cause of Christ because they go forward when others will not, ask God for what is needed and trust him for his provision.

GROUP 2: *Spiritual Gifts Matching*

	10	11	12
SPIRITUAL GIFT	HEALING	HELPS	HOSPITALITY
MATCHES			
CONTRIBUTES			

J. The divine enablement to contribute money and resources to the work of the Lord with cheerfulness and liberality. It doesn't ask, "How much money do I give?" but "How much of God's money do I keep?" People with this gift: manage their finances and limit their lifestyle in order to give as much of their resources as possible, support ministry with sacrificial gifts to advance the kingdom, meet tangible needs that enable spiritual growth to occur and provide resources trusting God for his provision, may have a special ability to make money to further God's work.

K. The divine enablement to effectively communicate the gospel to unbelievers so they respond in faith and move toward discipleship. People with this gift: communicate the message of Christ with clarity and conviction, seek out opportunities to talk to unbelievers about spiritual matters, challenge unbelievers to faith and to become fully devoted followers of Christ, adapt their presentation of the gospel to connect with the individual's needs, seek opportunities to build relationships with unbelievers.

L. The divine enablement to be God's means for restoring people to wholeness. People with this gift: demonstrate the power of God; bring restoration to the sick and diseased; authenticate a message from God through various kinds of healings; use it as an opportunity to communicate a biblical truth and to see God glorified; pray, touch, or speak words that miraculously bring healing to one's body, soul, or spirit.

GROUP 3: *Spiritual Gifts Matching*

	13	14	15
SPIRITUAL GIFT	INTERCESSION	INTERPRETATION	KNOWLEDGE
MATCHES			
CONTRIBUTES			

M. The divine enablement to authenticate the ministry and message of Christ through supernatural interventions that glorify God. People with this gift: speak God's truth and it is authenticated by an accompanying miracle that points people to a relationship with Jesus, express confidence in God's faithfulness, believe that God will manifest his presence, bring the ministry and message of Jesus Christ with power, claim God to be the source of the miracle and glorify God.

N. The divine enablement to consistently pray on behalf of and for others, seeing frequent and specific results. People with this gift: feel compelled to earnestly pray on behalf of someone or some cause, have a daily awareness of the spiritual battles being waged and pray, are convinced God moves in direct response to prayer, follow the leading of the Holy Spirit whether they understand it or not, exercise authority and power for the protection of others and the equipping of them for service.

O. The divine enablement to cast vision, motivate, and direct people to harmoniously accomplish the purposes of God. People with this gift: provide direction for God's people or ministries, inspire others to perform to the best of their abilities, present the "big picture" for others to see, model the values of the ministry, take responsibility to establish ministry goals.

GROUP 3: *Spiritual Gifts Matching*

	16	17	18
SPIRITUAL GIFT	LEADERSHIP	MERCY	MIRACLES
MATCHES			
CONTRIBUTES			

P. The divine enablement to bring truth to the body through a revelation or biblical insight. People with this gift: receive truth which enables them to better serve the body, search the Scriptures, understand truth, gain knowledge that at times is not attained by natural means but revealed to them by God, have an unusual insight or understanding that serves the church, communicate truth for teaching and practical use.

Q. The divine enablement to cheerfully and practically help those who are suffering or are in need. People with this gift: have compassion that moves them to action; focus on alleviating the sources of pain or discomfort in suffering people; address the needs of the lonely and forgotten; extend love, grace, and dignity to those facing hardships and crisis; serve in difficult or unsightly circumstances and do so with joy; concern themselves with individual or social issues that oppress people.

R. The divine enablement to make known to the body of Christ the message of one who is speaking in tongues. People with this gift: respond to a message spoken in tongues by giving an interpretation, glorify God and demonstrate his power through this miraculous manifestation, edify the body by interpreting a timely message from God, and can be prophetic.

GROUP 4: *Spiritual Gifts Matching*

	19	20	21
SPIRITUAL GIFT	PROPHECY	SHEPHERDING	TEACHING
MATCHES			
CONTRIBUTES			

S. The divine enablement to understand, clearly explain, and apply the Word of God causing greater Christlikeness in the lives of listeners. People with this gift: communicate biblical truth that inspires greater obedience to the Word, challenge listeners simply and practically with the truths of Scripture, teach the whole counsel of God for maximum life-change, give attention to detail and accuracy, prepare through extended times of study and reflection.

T. The divine enablement to nurture, care for, and guide people toward ongoing spiritual maturity and becoming like Christ. People with this gift: take responsibility to nurture the whole person in their walk with God, provide guidance and oversight to a group of God's people, model with their life what it means to be a fully devoted follower of Jesus, establish trust and confidence through long-term relationships, lead and protect those within their span of care.

U. The divine enablement to effectively apply spiritual truth to meet a need in a specific situation. People with this gift: focus on the unseen consequences in determining the next steps to take, receive an understanding of what is necessary to meet the needs of the body, provide divinely given solutions in the midst of conflicts and confusion, hear the Spirit provide direction for God's best, apply spiritual truth in practical ways.

GROUP 4: *Spiritual Gifts Matching*

	22	**23**
SPIRITUAL GIFT	**TONGUES**	**WISDOM**
MATCHES		
CONTRIBUTES		

V. The divine enablement to speak to the church in an unknown language. People with this gift: receive a spontaneous message from God which is made known to the body through the gift of interpretation, express a word by the Spirit to edify the church, speak in a language they have not learned and do not understand, are available to be used by God to speak to his church.

W. The divine enablement to reveal truth and proclaim it in a timely and relevant manner for understanding, correction, repentance, or edification. There can be immediate or future implications. People with this gift: expose sin or deception in others for the purpose of reconciliation, see truth that others often fail to see and challenge them to respond, warn of God's judgment if there is no repentance, understand God's heart and ministry through the experiences he takes them through.

Spiritual Gifts are NOT

- Natural talents

    like cooking, sports, singing, etc.

- The Fruit of the Spirit

    like love, joy, peace, etc.

- Church positions

    like pastor, Sunday school teacher, small group leader, etc.

- Christian disciplines

    like fasting, prayer, study, tithing, etc.

(See Appendix D on page 153 for more details.)

ASSIGNMENT: SPIRITUAL GIFTS ASSESSMENTS

Be sure to complete the following for next time:

- *Experience Assessment* (pages 53–64)

- *Observation Assessment* (pages 65–67)

- *Spiritual Gifts Summary* (page 68)

SPIRITUAL GIFTS DISCOVERY

Experience Assessment

Directions

1. Turn to page 55 and respond to each statement on the *Experience Assessment* that follows.

2. Place your score to each statement in the appropriate box on your answer sheet on page 54. Use the following scale:

SCORE		MEANING
3	=	Consistently / Definitely True
2	=	Most of the Time / Usually True
1	=	Some of the Time / Once in a While
0	=	Never / Not at All

3. **IMPORTANT:**

   - Answer according to who you are, not who you would like to be or think you should be.
   - How true are these statements of you?
   - What has been your experience?
   - To what degree do these statement reflect your tendencies?

4. When you have completed the *Experience Assessment*, add up each of the columns for a total above each letter.

1	2	3	4	5	6	7	8	9	10	11	12	13	14	15	16	17	18	19				
20	21	22	23	24	25	26	27	28	29	30	31	32	33	34	35	36	37	38				
39	40	41	42	43	44	45	46	47	48	49	50	51	52	53	54	55	56	57				
58	59	60	61	62	63	64	65	66	67	68	69	70	71	72	73	74	75	76				
77	78	79	80	81	82	83	84	85	86	87	88	89	90	91	92	93	94	95				
96	97	98	99	100	101	102	103	104	105	106	107	108	109	110	111	112	113	114				
115	116	117	118	119	120	121	122	123	124	125	126	127	128	129	130	131	132	133	134	135	136	137
A	B	C	D	E	F	G	H	I	J	K	L	M	N	O	P	Q	R	S	T	U	V	W

TOTAL

TOP GIFTS

INDICATE TOP 3 GIFTS: 1, 2, 3

IF MORE CONVENIENT, TEAR OUT HERE

SPIRITUAL GIFTS *EXPERIENCE ASSESSMENT*

1. I can coordinate people, tasks, and events to meet a need.

2. I enjoy working creatively with wood, cloth, paints, metal, glass, or other materials.

3. I enjoy developing and using my artistic skills (art, drama, music, photography, etc.).

4. When I see spiritual complacency, I am willing to challenge it.

5. I have confidence that God not only can, but he will.

6. I give liberally and joyfully to people in financial need or to projects requiring support.

7. I enjoy working behind the scenes to support the work of others.

8. I view my home as a safe and caring place to minister to people.

9. When it comes to my attention, I am honored to regularly pray for someone or for a concern.

10. I am motivated to set goals and influence others to achieve a vision in order to advance God's work on earth.

11. I empathize with hurting people and desire to help in their healing process.

12. I am attracted to the idea of serving in another country or an ethnic community.

13. I have spoken a timely and important prophetic word to others that I felt came to me directly from God while in prayer.

14. I have the ability to communicate the gospel with clarity and conviction.

15. I establish trust and confidence through long-term relationships.

16. I am able to communicate God's Word effectively.

17. I can readily distinguish between spiritual truth and error, good and evil.

18. I research and am persistent in my pursuit of knowing the truth.

19. Others often seek me out for advice about personal and spiritual matters.

20. I am careful, thorough, and skilled at managing details.

21. I am skilled in working with different kinds of tools.

22. I help people better understand themselves, their relationships, and God through artistic expression.

23. I enjoy reassuring and strengthening those who are discouraged.

24. I have confidence in God's continuing provision and help, even in difficult times.

25. I give more than a tithe so that kingdom work can be accomplished.

26. I enjoy doing routine tasks that support the needs of ministry.

27. I enjoy meeting new people and helping them feel welcomed.

28. I enjoy praying for long periods of time and receive leadings as to what God wants me to pray for.

29. It is quite natural for me to lead, and it is more comfortable for me to lead than not to lead.

30. I can patiently support those going through painful experiences as they are seeking stability in their lives.

31. I am willing to take an active part in starting a new church.

32. By God's revelation to me, I have been able to shed light on current realities in someone's life that helps them see God's desire for their future.

33. After I have shared the story of Jesus, people pray with me for salvation.

34. I can faithfully provide long-term emotional and spiritual support and concern for others.

35. I simply and practically explain and clarify the Word for those who are confused or just do not know.

36. I have a "sixth sense" and frequently am able to identify a person's character based on first impressions.

37. I receive information from the Spirit that I did not acquire through natural means.

38. I can often find simple, practical solutions in the midst of conflict or confusion.

39. I can clarify goals and develop strategies or plans to accomplish them.

40. I can visualize how something should be constructed before I build it.

41. I like finding new and fresh ways of communicating God's truth.

42. I give hope to others by directing them to the promises of God.

43. I have a special ability to trust God for extraordinary needs.

44. I manage my money well in order to free more of it for giving.

45. I willingly take on a variety of odd jobs around the church to meet the needs of others.

46. I genuinely believe the Lord directs strangers to me who need a sense of belonging and connection to others.

47. I am conscious of ministering to others as I pray.

48. I am usually chosen as the group's spokesperson when in discussion groups.

49. I am drawn toward people who are sometimes regarded as undeserving or beyond help.

50. I can relate to others in culturally sensitive ways.

51. I speak biblical truth in a timely and culturally sensitive way in order to strengthen, encourage, and comfort God's people.

52. I'd rather be around non-Christians more than Christians so that I can build relationships with them.

53. I enjoy giving practical support, nurture, and spiritual guidance to a group of people.

54. When I teach, people respond to my teaching with action.

55. I can see through phoniness or deceit before it is evident to others.

56. I seek certainty and truth in order to avoid superficial understandings and speculation.

57. I am surprised by how many people are unable to solve problems and seem to lack common sense.

58. I can identify and effectively use the resources needed to accomplish tasks.

59. I am good at working with my hands and enjoy doing so.

60. I regularly need to get alone to reflect and to develop my imagination.

61. I reassure those who need to take courageous action in their faith, family, or life.

62. I am unwavering in my belief that God will absolutely work in circumstances in which success cannot be guaranteed by human effort alone.

63. I choose to limit my lifestyle in order to give away a higher percentage of my income.

64. I see spiritual significance in doing practical tasks.

65. I rarely meet people I do not like and wouldn't want to see included in the life of the church.

66. I pray with confidence because I know that God works in response to prayer.

67. I set goals and direct people to effectively accomplish them.

68. I have great compassion for hurting people.

69. I view the overall picture and do not get hindered with problems along the way.

70. I have spoken to others about future events or situations that God revealed to me, and they happened as I said they would.

71. I boldly speak about salvation through Jesus Christ and see a positive response in those who are listening.

72. I can gently restore wandering believers to faith and fellowship.

73. I get frustrated when I see people's lack of biblical knowledge.

74. God shows me the difference between a demonic influence, a mental illness, and an error in truth.

75. When reading or studying Scripture, I see important biblical truths and themes that benefit others in the body of Christ.

76. I can anticipate the likely consequences of the actions of an individual or a group.

77. I like to help groups become more efficient.

78. I serve and work more behind the scenes to make things that are useful for ministry and that honor God.

79. The way I say and do things awakens the truth in others, so they say, "I have never thought of it that way."

80. I find great joy in affirming the value and worth of others.

81. When I see God's activity, I move toward it in spite of opposition or a lack of support.

82. For special projects and capital campaigns, I like to give in a way that encourages and inspires others to give generously.

83. I like to find things that need to be done and often do them without being asked.

84. For me, the greatest times of joy in the church are times of social interaction and fellowship.

85. When I hear about needy situations, I feel burdened to pray.

86. I influence others to perform to the best of their ability.

87. I look through a person's handicaps or problems to see a life that matters to God and an opportunity to serve.

88. I am culturally sensitive and comfortable with different ethnic groups.

89. I feel a compulsion to speak the words God gives me to strengthen, encourage, and comfort others.

90. I openly tell people that I am a Christian and want them to ask me about my faith.

91. There are a number of people in my life that I am personally guiding with truth, encouragement, caring, and wisdom.

92. I communicate Scripture in ways that cause others to learn and become motivated toward greater growth.

93. I receive affirmation from others concerning the reliability of my insights about them and of perceptions I have of others.

94. I have suddenly known things about others, but did not know how I knew them.

95. I give practical advice to help others through complicated situations.

96. I can visualize a coming event, anticipate potential problems, and develop strategies to meet them.

97. I am a resourceful person, able to find the best materials and tools required to build what is needed.

98. I use various forms of the arts to draw people closer to God and to his truth.

99. I like motivating others to take steps for spiritual growth.

100. I am regularly challenging others to trust God.

101. I manage my money and give to ministries that are well led and are making a difference for Christ in the lives of people.

102. I show my love for others in actions more than words.

103. I do whatever I can to make visitors and others feel they belong.

104. God gives me a peace and confidence that my prayers are being answered, even when I cannot see the results.

105. I am able to cast a vision for ministry that others want to follow and be a part of.

106. I enjoy bringing hope, joy, and comfort to people working through a crisis or chronic situation in their lives.

107. I relate to leaders who often follow me into new ministry ventures.

108. God reveals to me things others cannot see so when I speak to them they can understand his activity in their lives.

109. I love unchurched people no matter where they are on their spiritual journey.

110. I take responsibility to nurture the whole person in his or her walk with God.

111. I can present information and skills to others in ways that make it easier for them to grasp and apply them to their lives.

112. I have seen into the spiritual realm where spirits have been revealed to me by God.

113. The truths I learn and the understandings I gain create a burden for me because of the responsibility I feel to handle the information wisely.

114. When faced with how to apply biblical truths practically in a difficult or complex situation, God reveals to me a solution.

115. I want to bring order where there is organizational chaos.

116. I have good hand-eye coordination and good dexterity.

117. I have a sense of the whole and can creatively put things together in a harmonious flow that artistically communicates a biblical truth.

118. I carefully challenge or rebuke others in order to help them grow spiritually.

119. I find it natural to believe in God for things that others see as impossible.

120. I believe I have been given an abundance of resources so that I may give more to the Lord's work.

121. When a task needs to be done, I find it difficult to say no.

122. I can make people feel at ease even in unfamiliar surroundings.

123. I see specific results in direct response to my prayers.

124. I figure out where we need to go and help others to get there.

125. I am moved with compassion and motivated to remove the sources of another's sufferings.

126. God's authority and power are manifested in the new churches and ministries I served to start.

127. I feel compelled to expose sin wherever I see it and to challenge people to repentance.

128. I'm constantly thinking of ways to bring up spiritual matters with friends who do not know God.

129. I feel responsible to help oversee and protect believers from the things that keep them from fellowship with God and one another.

130. I struggle with how to take what I have been studying and communicate only those things that will help God's people learn what they need at the moment.

131. I can sense when demonic forces are at work in a person or situation.

132. I love learning and share with those who want to learn.

133. I like to read and study the book of Proverbs for its simple and powerful truths expressed in a clear and practical way.

If you have repeatedly had any of the following experiences, simply place a check mark in the appropriate box on the answer sheet.

134. I have repeatedly seen an instant healing as I laid hands on someone and prayed.

135. When I hear people speak in tongues, I feel the Spirit revealing his message to me, and I speak it aloud, interpreting it for the church.

136. I have experienced the power of God within me to cast out demons and heal the sick, and I see his supernatural intervention in nature.

137. I have spoken in a language I do not understand, and someone has spoken out to interpret what I had just said.

EXPERIENCE ASSESSMENT
KEY

A	Administration
B	Craftsmanship
C	Creative Communication
D	Encouragement
E	Faith
F	Giving
G	Helps
H	Hospitality
I	Intercession
J	Leadership
K	Mercy
L	Apostleship
M	Prophecy
N	Evangelism
O	Shepherding
P	Teaching
Q	Discernment
R	Word of Knowledge
S	Word of Wisdom
T	Healing
U	Interpretation
V	Miracles
W	Tongues
Other	

OBSERVATION ASSESSMENT

Spiritual Gifts Discovery

Often, you will not be aware of what others have appreciated about you or noticed about your abilities in ministry situations. This assessment gives people who know you an opportunity to affirm areas of possible Spiritual Giftedness.

Directions

1. Your Participant's Guide has three identical assessments (page 168). Remove them from your book and give an *Observation Assessment* to three people. Ask them to complete it and return it to you.

2. The best people to ask are Christians who have seen you involved in a ministry context. If this is not possible, ask people who know you well and can share observations from their knowledge and relationship with you.

3. Get started with these assessments right away. People will need time to fill them out and get them back to you for the next session.

4. When you have received your *Observation Assessments* back, compile them on the Observation Summary in your Participant's Guide on page 66.

5. Transfer your conclusions to the *Spiritual Gifts Summary* on page 68.

OBSERVATION ASSESSMENT

Spiritual Gifts Discovery

1. In chart below, put an "X" in the box by each of the top three Spiritual Gifts identified in each of your *Observation Assessments*.

	SPIRITUAL GIFT	OBSERVER 1	OBSERVER 2	OBSERVER 3	TOTAL	TOP GIFTS
A	Administration					
B	Craftsmanship					
C	Creative Comm.					
D	Encouragement					
E	Faith					
F	Giving					
G	Helps					
H	Hospitality					
I	Intercession					
J	Leadership					
K	Mercy					
L	Apostleship					
M	Prophecy					
N	Evangelism					
O	Shepherding					
P	Teaching					
Q	Discernment					
R	Knowledge					
S	Wisdom					
T	Healing					
U	Interpretation					
V	Miracles					
W	Tongues					

Remember, their perceptions will be affected by how long they have known you and the type of relationship they have with you (family, small group, work, neighborhood, ministry, etc.). Weigh these factors as you record and evaluate their responses. Give more weight to those who have seen you in ministry.

2. Add across the row to total each Spiritual Gift.

3. In the shaded column to the right, put a 1, 2, or 3 next to the three Spiritual Gifts identified with the highest total.

4. Transfer these top three Gifts to the Spiritual Gifts Summary on page 68.

SPIRITUAL GIFTS SUMMARY
Spiritual Gifts Discovery

Use this page to compile the results of your *Experience Assessment* and *Observation Assessments*.

EXPERIENCE ASSESSMENT	*OBSERVATION ASSESSMENTS*
What are the top Spiritual Gifts you identified on your *Experience Assessment?* (from page 54)	What Spiritual Gifts were most observed by those who know you well? (from page 66)
_____ _____ _____ _____	_____ _____ _____ _____

Now ... combine the results from both assessments into a list of what you think at this time are your top three, or primary, Spiritual Gifts.

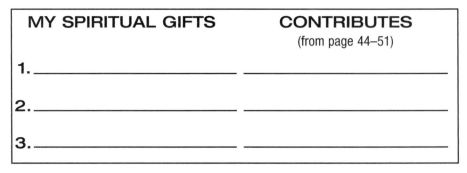

MY SPIRITUAL GIFTS	CONTRIBUTES (from page 44–51)
1. _____	_____
2. _____	_____
3. _____	_____

"The Discovery of Gifts"

Now about spiritual gifts, brothers, I do not want you to be ignorant.

1 Corinthians 12:1

As each one has received a special gift, employ it in serving one another as good stewards of the manifold grace of God.

1 Peter 4:10 NASB

INTRODUCTION

We've . . .

- Defined a Spiritual Gift

- Listed the Gifts from Scripture

- Matched them with their descriptions

- Seen their unique contributions and taken assessments to identify our own Spiritual Gifts

Now about spiritual gifts, brothers, I do not want you to be ignorant.

1 Corinthians 12:1

The true and final test of your Spiritual Gift comes through the AFFIRMATION *of the body of Christ.*

DVD VIGNETTE: SPIRITUAL GIFTS IN ACTION

Directions

1. As you watch the DVD, see if you can identify which Spiritual Gift each person has.

2. Write each Spiritual Gift you identify in the space below.

Tony _____

Jessie _____

Damarco _____

Ashley _____

Kayla _____

Nick _____

REFERENCE ASSESSMENT

Directions

This is an individual activity.

1. Locate your top Spiritual Gift in the *Reference Assessment*. All the gifts are listed alphabetically.

2. As you read through the information about your Spiritual Gift, put a check in the box by any item under Distinctives, Traits, or Cautions you feel applies to you. If you begin to sense that the items are not particularly descriptive of you, take a look at what you've identified as your second possible gift. See if there is a better match.

3. If you finish before time is up, look up the Scripture passages at the bottom of the page or read about the next gift on your list.

ADMINISTRATION

Literal Meaning: To pilot or steer a ship

Description: The gift of Administration is the divine enablement to understand what makes an organization function, and the special ability to plan and execute procedures that accomplish the goals of the ministry.

Distinctives:
- Develop strategies or plans to reach identified goals
- Assist ministries to become more effective and efficient
- Create order out of organizational chaos
- Manage or coordinate a variety of responsibilities to accomplish a task
- Organize people, tasks, or events

Traits:
- Thorough
- Objective
- Responsible
- Organized
- Goal-oriented
- Efficient
- Conscientious

Cautions:
- Need to be open to adjusting their plans, so that they don't stifle a leader's vision
- Could use people simply to accomplish goals without being concerned for their growth in the process
- Could fail to see God's purposes being fulfilled in the process of meeting a goal

References: 1 Corinthians 12:28; Acts 6:1–7; Exodus 18:13–26

APOSTLESHIP

Literal Meaning: To be sent with a message

Description: The gift of Apostleship is the divine ability to start and oversee the development of new churches or ministry structures.

Distinctives:
❏ Pioneer and establish new ministries or churches
❏ Adapt to different surroundings by being culturally sensitive and aware
❏ Desire to minister to unreached people in other communities or countries
❏ Have responsibilities to oversee ministries or groups of churches
❏ Demonstrate authority and vision for the mission of the church

Traits:
❏ Adventurous
❏ Entrepreneurial
❏ Persevering
❏ Adaptable
❏ Culturally sensitive
❏ Risk-taking
❏ Cause-driven

Cautions:
❏ Should be aware that misusing their authority can quench the Spirit in others
❏ Need to be affirmed and sent by the church
❏ Can be demanding and pessimistic

References: 1 Corinthians 12:28–29; Ephesians 4:11–12; Romans 1:5; Acts 13:2–3

CRAFTSMANSHIP

Literal Meaning: To craft, design, build

Description: The gift of Craftsmanship is the divine enablement to creatively design and/or construct items to be used for ministry.

Distinctives:
- ❏ Work with wood, cloth, paints, metal, glass, and other raw materials
- ❏ Make things that increase the effectiveness of others' ministries
- ❏ Enjoy serving with their hands to meet tangible needs
- ❏ Design and build tangible items and resources for ministry use
- ❏ Work with different kinds of tools and are skilled with their hands

Traits:
- ❏ Creative
- ❏ Designer
- ❏ Handy
- ❏ Resourceful
- ❏ Practical
- ❏ Behind-the-scenes
- ❏ Helpful

Cautions:
- ❏ Could fail to see that their gift is significant and one that makes a spiritual contribution to the body
- ❏ Could use people to get things done instead of helping them grow in the process
- ❏ Should remember that the things they produce are just a means to the end and not the end itself

References: Exodus 31:3; 35:31–35; Acts 9:36–39; 2 Kings 22:5–6

CREATIVE COMMUNICATION

Literal Meaning: To communicate artistically

Description: The gift of Creative Communication is the divine enablement to communicate God's truth through a variety of art forms.

Distinctives:
- ❏ Use the arts to communicate God's truth
- ❏ Develop and use artistic skills such as drama, writing, art, music, etc.
- ❏ Use variety and creativity to captivate people and cause them to consider Christ's message
- ❏ Challenge people's perspective of God through various forms of the arts
- ❏ Demonstrate fresh ways to express the Lord's ministry and message

Traits:
- ❏ Expressive
- ❏ Imaginative
- ❏ Idea-oriented
- ❏ Artistic
- ❏ Creative
- ❏ Unconventional
- ❏ Sensitive

Cautions:
- ❏ Need to remember that art is not for art's sake, but it's to glorify God and edify others
- ❏ Could find evaluation and constructive criticism difficult to accept
- ❏ Might be uncooperative (because of ego, pride, or individualism) and need to work at being a team player

References: Psalms 150:3–5; 2 Samuel 6:14–15; Mark 4:2, 33

DISCERNMENT

Literal Meaning: To separate or make a distinction, differentiate

Description: The gift of Discernment (of spirits) is the divine enablement to distinguish between truth and error. It is able to discern the spirits, differentiating between good and evil, right and wrong.

Distinctives:
- ❏ Distinguish truth from error, right from wrong, pure motives from impure
- ❏ Identify deception in others with accuracy and appropriateness
- ❏ Determine whether a word attributed to God is authentic
- ❏ Recognize inconsistencies in a teaching, prophetic message, or interpretation
- ❏ Are able to sense the presence of evil

Traits:
- ❏ Perceptive
- ❏ Insightful
- ❏ Sensitive
- ❏ Intuitive
- ❏ Decisive
- ❏ Challenging
- ❏ Truthful

Cautions:
- ❏ May struggle with how to express their perceptions, feelings, or insights
- ❏ Could be harsh when confronting others, instead of speaking the truth in love
- ❏ Need to confirm their perceptions before speaking

References: 1 Corinthians 12:10; Acts 5:1–4; Matthew 16:21–23

ENCOURAGEMENT

Literal Meaning: To come alongside of

Description: The gift of Encouragement is the divine enablement to present truth so as to strengthen, comfort, or urge to action those who are discouraged or wavering in their faith.

Distinctives:
- ❏ Come to the side of those who are discouraged to strengthen and reassure them
- ❏ Challenge, comfort, or confront others to trust and hope in the promises of God
- ❏ Urge others to action by applying biblical truth
- ❏ Motivate others to grow
- ❏ Emphasize God's promises and have confidence in his will

Traits:
- ❏ Positive
- ❏ Motivating
- ❏ Challenging
- ❏ Affirming
- ❏ Reassuring
- ❏ Supportive
- ❏ Trustworthy

Cautions:
- ❏ Can sometimes be overly optimistic, too simplistic, or flattering
- ❏ Should first take time to understand where others are and what they really need
- ❏ May want to just say "positive" things to others and avoid being confrontational when it's needed

References: Romans 12:8; Acts 11:22–24; 15:30–32

EVANGELISM

Literal Meaning: To bring good news

Description: The gift of Evangelism is the divine enablement to effectively communicate the gospel to unbelievers so they respond in faith and move toward discipleship.

Distinctives:
- ❏ Communicate the message of Christ with clarity and conviction
- ❏ Seek out opportunities to talk to unbelievers about spiritual matters
- ❏ Challenge unbelievers to faith and to become fully devoted followers of Christ
- ❏ Adapt their presentation of the gospel to connect with the individual's needs
- ❏ Seek opportunities to build relationships with unbelievers

Traits:
- ❏ Sincere/Serious
- ❏ Candid
- ❏ Respected
- ❏ Influential
- ❏ Spiritual
- ❏ Confident
- ❏ Commitment-oriented

Cautions:
- ❏ Need to remember the Holy Spirit, not guilt, is the motivator in a person's decision for Christ
- ❏ Should avoid becoming critical of others by remembering that we are all "witnesses," but we are not all "evangelists"
- ❏ Need to listen to people carefully, because the same approach is not appropriate for everyone

References: Ephesians 4:11; Acts 8:26–40; Luke 19:1–10

FAITH

Literal Meaning: To trust, have confidence, believe

Description: The gift of Faith is the divine enablement to act on God's promises with confidence and unwavering belief in God's ability to fulfill his purposes.

Distinctives:
- ❏ Believe the promises of God and inspire others to do the same
- ❏ Act in complete confidence of God's ability to overcome obstacles
- ❏ Demonstrate an attitude of trust in God's will and his promises
- ❏ Advance the cause of Christ because they go forward when others will not
- ❏ Ask God for what is needed and trust him for his provision

Traits:
- ❏ Prayerful
- ❏ Optimistic
- ❏ Trusting
- ❏ Assured
- ❏ Positive
- ❏ Inspiring
- ❏ Hopeful

Cautions:
- ❏ Need to act on their faith
- ❏ Should remember that those who speak with reason and desire to plan do not necessarily lack faith
- ❏ Should listen to and consider the counsel of wise and Spirit-filled believers

References: 1 Corinthians 12:9; 13:2; Hebrews 11:1; Romans 4:18–21

GIVING

Literal Meaning: To give part of, share

Description: The gift of Giving is the divine enablement to contribute money and resources to the work of the Lord with cheerfulness and liberality. People with this gift do not ask, "How much money do I need to give to God?" but "How much money do I need to live on?"

Distinctives:
- ❏ Manage their finances and limit their lifestyle in order to give as much of their resources as possible
- ❏ Support the work of ministry with sacrificial gifts to advance the kingdom
- ❏ Meet tangible needs that enable spiritual growth to occur
- ❏ Provide resources, generously and cheerfully, trusting God for his provision
- ❏ May have a special ability to make money so that they may use it to further God's work

Traits:
- ❏ Stewardship-oriented
- ❏ Responsible
- ❏ Resourceful
- ❏ Charitable
- ❏ Trusts in God
- ❏ Disciplined

Cautions:
- ❏ Need to esteem their gift, remembering that giving money and resources is a spiritual contribution to the body of Christ
- ❏ Need to remember the church's agenda is determined by leaders, not by the giver's gift
- ❏ Need to guard against greed

References: Romans 12:8; 2 Corinthians 6:8; Luke 21:1–4

HEALING

Literal Meaning: To restore instantaneously

Description: The gift of Healing(s) is the divine enablement to be God's means for restoring people to wholeness.

NOTE: The Greek word is actually plural, "healings," which indicate that different kinds of healings are possible with this gift (i.e., emotional, relational, spiritual, physical, etc.).

Distinctives:
- ❏ Demonstrate the power of God
- ❏ Bring restoration to the sick and diseased
- ❏ Authenticate a message from God through healing
- ❏ Use healing as an opportunity to communicate a biblical truth and to see God glorified
- ❏ Pray, touch, or speak words that miraculously bring healing to one's body

Traits:
- ❏ Compassionate
- ❏ Trusts in God
- ❏ Prayerful
- ❏ Full of faith
- ❏ Humble
- ❏ Responsive
- ❏ Obedient

Cautions:
- ❏ Need to remember that it is not always their faith or the faith of the sick that determines a healing, but God who determines it
- ❏ Need to realize that God does not promise to heal everyone who asks or is prayed for
- ❏ Should remember that Jesus did not heal everyone who was sick or suffering while he was on the earth

References: 1 Corinthians 12:9, 28, 30; Acts 3:1–16; Mark 2:1–12

HELPS

Literal Meaning: To take the place of someone

Description: The gift of Helps is the divine enablement to accomplish practical and necessary tasks which free up, support, and meet the needs of others.

Distinctives:
- Serve behind the scenes wherever needed to support the gifts and ministries of others
- Seek the tangible and practical things to be done and enjoy doing them
- Sense God's purpose and pleasure in meeting everyday responsibilities
- Attach spiritual value to practical service
- Enjoy knowing that they are freeing up others to do what God has called them to do

Traits:
- Available
- Willing
- Helpful
- Reliable
- Loyal
- Dependable
- Whatever-it-takes attitude

Cautions:
- Need to esteem their gift, remembering that doing practical deeds is a *spiritual* contribution to the body of Christ
- Find it difficult to say "no"
- Need to be responsive to the priorities of leadership instead of setting their own agendas

References: 1 Corinthians 12:28; Romans 12:7; Acts 6:1–4; Romans 16:1–2

HOSPITALITY

Literal Meaning: To love strangers

Description: The gift of Hospitality is the divine enablement to care for people by providing fellowship, food, and shelter.

Distinctives:
- ❏ Provide an environment where people feel valued and cared for
- ❏ Meet new people and help them to feel welcomed
- ❏ Create a safe and comfortable setting where relationships can develop
- ❏ Seek ways to connect people together into meaningful relationships
- ❏ Set people at ease in unfamiliar surroundings

Traits:
- ❏ Friendly
- ❏ Gracious
- ❏ Inviting
- ❏ Trusting
- ❏ Caring
- ❏ Responsive
- ❏ Warm

Cautions:
- ❏ Should avoid viewing their gift as just "entertaining"
- ❏ Need to remember to ask *God* who he wants them to befriend and serve
- ❏ Should be careful not to cause stress in their own family when inviting others into their home

References: 1 Peter 4:9–10; Romans 12:13; Hebrews 13:1–2

INTERCESSION

Literal Meaning: To plead on behalf of someone, intercede

Description: The gift of Intercession is the divine enablement to consistently pray on behalf of and for others, seeing frequent and specific results.

Distinctives:
- ❏ Feel compelled to earnestly pray on behalf of someone or some cause
- ❏ Have a daily awareness of the spiritual battles being waged and pray
- ❏ Are convinced God moves in direct response to prayer
- ❏ Pray in response to the leading of the Spirit, whether they understand it or not
- ❏ Exercise authority and power for the protection of others and the equipping of them to serve

Traits:
- ❏ Advocate
- ❏ Caring
- ❏ Sincere
- ❏ Peacemaker
- ❏ Trustworthy
- ❏ Burden bearer
- ❏ Spiritually sensitive

Cautions:
- ❏ Should avoid feeling that their gift is not valued, by remembering that interceding for others is their ministry and spiritual contribution- to the body of Christ
- ❏ Should avoid using prayer as an escape from fulfilling responsibilities
- ❏ Need to avoid a "holier-than-thou" attitude sometimes caused by extended times of prayer and spiritual intimacy with God

References: Romans 8:26–27; John 17:9–26; 1 Timothy 2:1–2; Colossians 1:9–12; 4:12–13

INTERPRETATION

Literal Meaning: To translate, interpret

Description: The gift of Interpretation is the divine enablement to make known to the body of Christ the message of one who is speaking in tongues.

Distinctives:
- ❏ Respond to a message spoken in tongues by giving an interpretation
- ❏ Glorify God and demonstrate his power through this miraculous manifestation
- ❏ Edify the body by interpreting a timely message from God
- ❏ Understand an unlearned language and communicate that message to the body of Christ
- ❏ Are sometimes prophetic when exercising an interpretation of tongues for the church

Traits:
- ❏ Worshipful
- ❏ Responsive
- ❏ Devoted
- ❏ Responsible
- ❏ Spiritually intimate
- ❏ Sensitive
- ❏ Faithful

Cautions:
- ❏ Need to remember that the message being interpreted should reflect the will of God and not man
- ❏ Should remember that this gift is to provide edification, it's to build up the church
- ❏ Use it in an orderly manner in conjunction with tongues

References: 1 Corinthians 12:10; 14:5, 26–28

Word of KNOWLEDGE

Literal Meaning: To know

Description: The gift of the Word of Knowledge is the divine enablement to bring truth to the body through a revelation or biblical insight.

Distinctives:
- ❏ Receive truth which enables them to better serve the body
- ❏ Search the Scriptures for insight, understanding, and truth
- ❏ Have an unusual insight or understanding that serves the church
- ❏ Organize information for teaching and practical use
- ❏ Gain knowledge which was not attained by natural observation or means

Traits:
- ❏ Inquisitive
- ❏ Responsive
- ❏ Observant
- ❏ Insightful
- ❏ Reflective
- ❏ Truthful
- ❏ Spiritually sensitive

Cautions:
- ❏ Need to be careful of this gift leading to pride ("knowledge" puffs up)
- ❏ Should remember that it's God's message, not theirs, when they give a word of knowledge to the church
- ❏ Need to remember with the increasing of knowing comes the increasing of pain (Ecclesiastes 1:18)

References: 1 Corinthians 12:8; Mark 2:6–8; John 1:45–50

LEADERSHIP

Literal Meaning: To stand before

Description: The gift of Leadership is the divine enablement to cast vision, motivate, and direct people to harmoniously accomplish the purposes of God.

Distinctives:
- ❏ Provide direction for God's people or ministry
- ❏ Motivate others to perform to the best of their abilities
- ❏ Present the "big picture" for others to see
- ❏ Model the values of the ministry
- ❏ Take responsibility and establish goals

Traits:
- ❏ Influential
- ❏ Diligent
- ❏ Visionary
- ❏ Trustworthy
- ❏ Persuasive
- ❏ Motivating
- ❏ Goal setter

Cautions:
- ❏ Should realize their relational credibility takes time and is critical for leadership effectiveness
- ❏ Should remember that servant leadership is the biblical model, the greatest being the servant of all
- ❏ Do not need to be in a leadership "position" to use this gift

References: Romans 12:8; Hebrews 13:17; Luke 22:25–26

MERCY

Literal Meaning: To have compassion

Description: The gift of Mercy is the divine enablement to cheerfully and practically help those who are suffering or in need, having compassion that is moved to action.

Distinctives:
- Focus upon alleviating the sources of pain or discomfort in suffering people
- Address the needs of the lonely and forgotten
- Extend love, grace, and dignity to those facing hardships and crisis
- Serve in difficult or unsightly circumstances and do so cheerfully
- Concern themselves with individual or social issues that oppress people

Traits:
- Empathetic
- Caring
- Responsive
- Kind
- Compassionate
- Sensitive
- Burden-bearing

Cautions:
- Need to be aware that rescuing people from their pain may be hindering God's work in them
- Need to guard against feeling "unappreciated," since some of the people helped will not show or express any appreciation
- Should guard against becoming defensive and angry about the sources of others' pain

References: Romans 12:8; Matthew 5:7; Mark 10:46–52; Luke 10:25–37

MIRACLES

Literal Meaning: To do powerful deeds

Description: The gift of Miracles is the divine enablement to authenticate the ministry and message of God through supernatural interventions which glorify him.

Distinctives:
- ❏ Speak God's truth and have it authenticated by an accompanying miracle
- ❏ Express confidence in God's faithfulness and ability to manifest his presence
- ❏ Bring the ministry and message of Jesus Christ with power
- ❏ Claim God to be the source of the miracle and glorify him
- ❏ Represent Christ and through the miracle, point people to a relationship with Christ

Traits:
- ❏ Bold
- ❏ Venturesome
- ❏ Authoritative
- ❏ God-fearing
- ❏ Convincing
- ❏ Prayerful
- ❏ Responsive

Cautions:
- ❏ Need to remember that miracles are not necessarily caused by faith
- ❏ Should avoid viewing this gift as a personal responsibility, remembering that God determines the location and timing of his deeds
- ❏ Need to guard against the temptation to call on the Lord's presence and power for selfish purposes

References: 1 Corinthians 12:10, 28–29; John 2:1–11; Luke 5:1–11

PROPHECY

Literal Meaning: To speak before

Description: The gift of Prophecy is the divine enablement to reveal truth and proclaim it in a timely and relevant manner for understanding, correction, repentance, or edification. There may be immediate or future implications.

Distinctives:
❏ Expose sin or deception in others for the purpose of reconciliation
❏ Speak a timely word from God causing conviction, repentance, and edification
❏ See truth that others often fail to see and challenge them to respond
❏ Warn of God's immediate or future judgment if there is no repentance
❏ Understand God's heart and mind through experiences he takes them through

Traits:
❏ Discerning
❏ Compelling
❏ Uncompromising
❏ Outspoken
❏ Authoritative
❏ Convicting
❏ Confronting

Cautions:
❏ Need to be aware that listeners may reject the message if it's not spoken in love and for their edification
❏ Need to avoid pride, which can create a demanding or discouraging spirit that hinders the gift
❏ Should remember that discernment and Scripture must support and agree with each prophecy

References: Romans 12:6; 1 Corinthians 12:10, 28; 13:2; 2 Peter 1:19–21

SHEPHERDING

Literal Meaning: To shepherd a flock

Description: The gift of Shepherding is the divine enablement to nurture, care for, and guide people toward ongoing spiritual maturity and becoming like Christ.

Distinctives:
- ❑ Take responsibility to nurture the whole person in their walk with God
- ❑ Provide guidance and oversight to a group of God's people
- ❑ Model with their life what it means to be a fully devoted follower of Jesus Christ
- ❑ Establish trust, loyalty, and confidence through long-term relationships
- ❑ Lead and protect those within their span of care

Traits:
- ❑ Influencing
- ❑ Nurturing
- ❑ Guiding
- ❑ Discipling
- ❑ Protective
- ❑ Supportive
- ❑ Relational

Cautions:
- ❑ Should remember that God judges those who neglect or abuse their oversight responsibilities
- ❑ Need to be aware that the desire to feed and support others can make it difficult to say "no"
- ❑ Should realize that some of those being nurtured will grow beyond the shepherd's own ability and need to be freed to do so

References: Ephesians 4:11–12; 1 Peter 5:1–4; John 10:1–18

TEACHING

Literal Meaning: To instruct

Description: The gift of Teaching is the divine enablement to understand, clearly explain, and apply the Word of God, causing greater Christlikeness in the lives of listeners.

Distinctives:
- ❑ Communicate biblical truth that inspires greater obedience to the Word
- ❑ Challenge listeners simply and practically with the truths of Scripture
- ❑ Present the whole counsel of God for maximum life-change
- ❑ Give attention to detail and accuracy
- ❑ Prepare through extended times of study and reflection

Traits:
- ❑ Disciplined
- ❑ Perceptive
- ❑ Teachable
- ❑ Authoritative
- ❑ Practical
- ❑ Analytical
- ❑ Articulate

Cautions:
- ❑ Should avoid pride that may result from their "superior" biblical knowledge and understanding
- ❑ Could become too detailed when teaching and fail to make life application
- ❑ Should remember that their spirituality is not measured by how much they know

References: Romans 12:7; 1 Corinthians 12:28–29; Acts 18:24–28; 2 Timothy 2:2

TONGUES

Literal Meaning: Tongue, language

Description: The gift of Tongues is the divine enablement to receive a spontaneous message from God in public worship and to speak it in an unknown language that is then made known to the church through the gift of interpretation.

Distinctives:
- ❏ Express with an interpretation a word by the Spirit which edifies the church
- ❏ Communicate a message given by God for the church
- ❏ Speak in a language they have never learned or do not understand
- ❏ Worship the Lord with unknown words too deep for the mind to comprehend
- ❏ Experience an intimacy with God which inspires them to serve and edify others

Traits:
- ❏ Worshipful
- ❏ Prayerful
- ❏ Responsive
- ❏ Trusting
- ❏ Devoted
- ❏ Spontaneous
- ❏ Receptive

Cautions:
- ❏ Should remain silent in the church if there is no gift of interpretation
- ❏ Should avoid expecting others to manifest this gift which may cause inauthenticity of the Spirit
- ❏ Should remember that all the gifts, including this one, are to edify others

References: 1 Corinthians 12:10, 28–30; 13:1; 14:1–33; Acts 2:1–11

Word of WISDOM

Literal Meaning: To apply truth practically

Description: The gift of Wisdom is the divine enablement to effectively apply spiritual truth to meet a need in a specific situation.

Distinctives:
- ❑ Focus on the unseen consequences in determining the next steps to take
- ❑ Receive an understanding of what is necessary to meet the needs of the body of Christ
- ❑ Provide divinely given solutions in the midst of conflict and confusion
- ❑ Hear the Spirit provide direction for God's best in a given situation
- ❑ Apply spiritual truth in specific and practical ways

Traits:
- ❑ Sensible
- ❑ Insightful
- ❑ Practical
- ❑ Wise
- ❑ Fair
- ❑ Experienced
- ❑ Common sense

Cautions:
- ❑ Could fail to share the wisdom that God has given them
- ❑ Need to avoid having others develop a dependence upon them, which may weaken their faith in God
- ❑ Need to be patient with others who do not have this gift

References: 1 Corinthians 12:8; 2:3–14; James 3:13–18; Jeremiah 9:23–24

95

GROUPS: CLARIFYING GIFTS

Directions

1. Form a group with two to three other people.

2. Further clarify your Spiritual Gift(s) by sharing with your group

    a. Your primary Spiritual Gift and why you think you have it.

    b. A caution you think you need to be aware of when using this Spiritual Gift.

3. Listen to others in your group as they share about their Spiritual Gifts to get a better understanding of how others see and use their gifts.

GENERAL CAUTIONS

The first caution is Gift __PROJECTION__.

> When a person projects his or her Spiritual
> Gift on others, that person is saying,
> "Do as I do."

The second caution is Gift Elevation.

> Gift Elevation says, "I have a more important
> Spiritual Gift than you."

THE ANIMAL STORY

SUMMARY

Some important truths:

- We are not to be ignorant or unaware about Spiritual Gifts.

- The true and final test of your Spiritual Gift comes through the affirmation of the body of Christ.

- Spiritual Gifts come with cautions. That is why we need to understand and develop our gifts.

- Your serving excels through the use of your Spiritual Gift.

"The Power of Love" and The Value of Personality"

And now I will show you the most excellent way.
1 Corinthians 12:31

All the days ordained for me were written in your book before one of them came to be.
Psalm 139:16

SERVING WITH LOVE

And now I will show you the most excellent way.

1 Corinthians 12:31

First Corinthians 12 lays the theological foundation for serving.

In 1 Corinthians 13, Paul talks about __LOVE__ as the way we are to serve one another!

1 Corinthians 13:1–3

*If I speak in the **tongues** of men and of angels,*	[Spiritual Gift]
but have not love,	[Lacking Love]
I am only a resounding gong or a clanging cymbal.	[No Impact]
*If I have the gift of **prophecy***	[Spiritual Gift]
*and can fathom all mysteries (**wisdom**)*	[Spiritual Gift]
*and all **knowledge**,*	[Spiritual Gift]
*and if I have a **faith** that can move mountains,*	[Spiritual Gift]
but have not love,	[Lacking Love]
I am nothing.	[No Impact]
*If I give all I possess to the poor (**voluntary poverty**)*	[Spiritual Gift]
*and surrender my body to the flames, (**martyrdom**)*	[Spiritual Gift]
but have not love,	[Lacking Love]
I gain nothing.	[No Impact]

Spiritual Gifts expressed without love . . .

- Do not reflect who God is.
- Do not have a __KINGDOM__ impact.

Love is . . .

Patient

Kind

Not envious

Not boastful

Not proud

Not rude

Not self-seeking

Not easily angered

Not keeping record of wrongs

Not delighting in evil

Rejoicing with the truth

Protecting

Always trusting

Always hoping

Always persevering

Never fails

1 Corinthians 13:4–8

SERVANTHOOD AND SERVILITY

	SERVANTHOOD *Serving **with** Love*	SERVILITY *Serving **without** Love*
A. Serves out of . . .	OBEDIENCE *"I want to serve God"*	OBLIGATION *"I have to serve God"*
B. Motivated by . . .	**What God Sees** *Serves an audience of One*	**What Others See** *Serves to please others*
C. Has attitude of . . .	**Whatever It Takes** *Goes beyond expectations*	**It's Not My Job** *Does the minimum*
D. Results are . . .	**God-Glorifying** *Directs attention to God* *Humbly reflecting Christ*	**Self-Seeking** *Draws attention to self* *Pridefully promoting self*

We are not to be "secret servants."

> *Let your light shine before men, that they may see your good deeds and praise [glorify] your Father in heaven.*
>
> Matthew 5:16

A visible act of service, done in love, makes a kingdom difference.

> *By this all men will know that you are my disciples, if you love one another.*
>
> John 13:35

We will not be known by our Spiritual Gifts, or by the things we do, but by the love we have for one another.

What does love have to do with serving?

___EVERYTHING___!

DVD VIGNETTE: SERVANTHOOD AND SERVILITY

Directions

1. Identify which people are displaying attitudes of servanthood or servility.

2. Identify how love is or is not being shown.

Character	Servanthood/ Servility	How?
Nick		
Ashley		
Kayla		

GROUPS: SERVANTHOOD

Directions

1. Form a group with two or three other people.

2. Each person discuss one aspect of servanthood (serving with love) that you would like to concentrate on.

3. Identify one practical step you want to take toward this goal.

One aspect of servanthood
I want to concentrate on as I serve is:

_____

_____

_____

One practical step I can take toward
greater servanthood is:

_____

_____

_____

SERVANT PROFILE: PERSONAL STYLE

Your Personal Style is your "personality" or "temperament."

Three truths about Personal Style:

1. Personal Style is God-given.

2. There is no right or wrong Personal Style. Personal Styles are just different.

3. Personal Style answers the "___HOW___" question: How can I best serve?

For you created my inmost being; you knit me together in my mother's womb. I praise you because I am fearfully and wonderfully made; your works are wonderful, I know that full well. My frame was not hidden from you when I was made in the secret place. When I was woven together in the depths of the earth, your eyes saw my unformed body. All the days ordained for me were written in your book before one of them came to be.

Psalm 139:13–16

PERSONAL STYLE ASSESSMENT

Directions

1. Read each statement and circle the number along the continuum that best describes what you would *prefer* to do or be. If you have a strong preference, circle a 1 or 5. If it is moderate, circle a 2 or 4. Remember, there are no right or wrong responses.

2. Do NOT answer according to what you feel is expected by a spouse, family member, church leader, or employer.

3. Select the behavior or perspective that would come most naturally to you if you knew there were no restrictions or consequences for your personal expression.

4. When you have completed your Assessment, total your "E" and "O" scores. Then turn to page 111 and plot your results on the graph provided. Notice where you are on the chart.

PERSONAL STYLE ASSESSMENT

How are you ENERGIZED?

1. I am more comfortable . . .

Doing things for people ← **1** — **2** — **3** — **4** — **5** → Being with people

2. When doing a task, I tend to . . .

Focus on the goal ← **1** — **2** — **3** — **4** — **5** → Focus on relationships

3. I get more excited about . . .

Advancing a cause ← **1** — **2** — **3** — **4** — **5** → Creating community

4. I feel I have accomplished something when I've . . .

Completed a job ← **1** — **2** — **3** — **4** — **5** → Built a relationship

5. It is more important to start a meeting . . .

On time ← **1** — **2** — **3** — **4** — **5** → When everyone gets there

6. I am more concerned with . . .

Meeting a deadline ← **1** — **2** — **3** — **4** — **5** → Maintaining the team

7. I place a higher value on . . .

Action ← **1** — **2** — **3** — **4** — **5** → Communication

How are you ENERGIZED?   **E=**   **TOTAL**

PERSONAL STYLE ASSESSMENT

How are you ORGANIZED?

1. In life, I generally prefer to ...

Be spontaneous ◄ **1 2 3 4 5** ► Follow a set plan

2. I prefer to set guidelines that are ...

General ◄ **1 2 3 4 5** ► Specific

3. I prefer to ...

Leave my options open ◄ **1 2 3 4 5** ► Settle things now

4. I prefer projects that have ...

Variety ◄ **1 2 3 4 5** ► Routine

5. I like to ...

Play it by ear ◄ **1 2 3 4 5** ► Stick to a plan

6. I find routine ...

Boring ◄ **1 2 3 4 5** ► Restful

7. I accomplish tasks best ...

By working it out as I go ◄ **1 2 3 4 5** ► By following a plan

How are you ORGANIZED? **0 =** [ ] **TOTAL**

PERSONAL STYLE ASSESSMENT

Finding Your Preferred Style

Use the graph on the next page:

1. Take the total number from your "O" scale (from page 109) and place an "X" where you find it along the horizontal line (Unstructured/Structured).

2. Take the total number from your "E" scale (from page 108) and place an "X" where you find it along the vertical line (Task-oriented/People-oriented).

3. Along the "O" scale, draw a line up and down through the "X" you placed there (see example below).

4. Along the "E" scale, draw a line across through the "X" you placed there (see example below).

5. Your Personal Style is indicated at the intersection point where the two lines cross (see example below).

EXAMPLE:

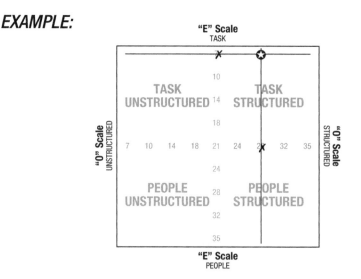

PERSONAL STYLE ASSESSMENT

Your Preferred Style

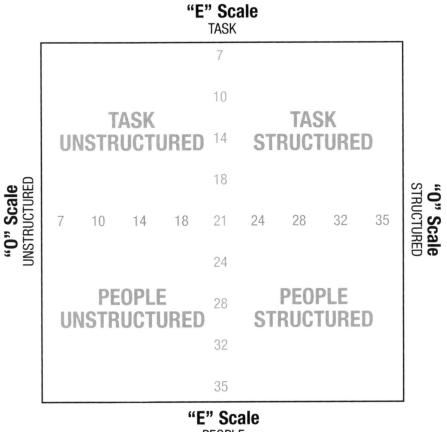

Which of the four Personal Styles do you have?

My Personal Style is

_____

(Task or People)   (Unstructured or Structured)

"The Influence of Passion"

For it is God who works in you to will and to act according to his good purpose.

Philippians 2:13

Delight yourself in the LORD and he will give you the desires of your heart.

Psalm 37:4

PERSONAL STYLE DESCRIPTION

PERSONAL STYLE

Personal Style indicates the way you prefer to relate to people and the world around you.

Serving in ways inconsistent with your Personal Style over time leads to

- Inauthentic relationships
- Decreased motivation
- Burnout

Two key elements of your Personal Style:

- How are you Energized?
- How are you Organized?

NOTE: If you are not sure of your Personal Style, refer back to the results of your *Personal Style Assessment* on page 111.

YOUR PERSONAL STYLE

1. How are you Energized?

- Reflects how you receive and focus your emotional energy
- Indicates how you prefer to interact with people and tasks

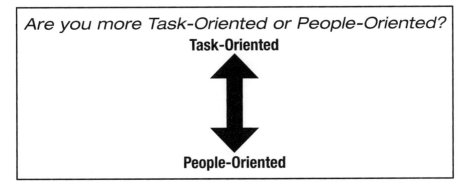

Are you more Task-Oriented or People-Oriented?

Task-Oriented

People-Oriented

Task-Oriented people:

- Are energized by
    doing things
    accomplishing tasks
    working with people who share your commitment
        to the task
- Can feel awkward or frustrated with a lot of relational activities

People-Oriented people:

- Are energized by
    interpersonal relationships
    people interactions
    working with people in a team setting
- Can feel awkward when handling a lot of tasks

BOTH value developing relationships and meeting goals!

2. How are you Organized?

- Reflects how you prefer to organize your world

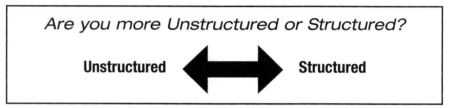

Are you more Unstructured or Structured?

Unstructured ⬅➡ **Structured**

Unstructured people:

- Put everything into *piles*
- Are less concerned with being precise
- Prefer lots of options and flexibility
- Prefer a variety of activities
- Are comfortable in undefined situations
- Like spontaneous relationships

Structured people:

- Put everything into *files*
- Plan and bring order to their lives
- Enjoy stable, consistent relationships
- Make decisions and seek closure
- Are more detailed
- Like things clearly defined

BOTH value being organized!

CAUTION

Personal Style does explain our behavior, but it does not

___EXCUSE___ it!

Task Unstructured

You tend to:

- Like general guidelines
- Be versatile
- Get tangible results
- Help wherever needed

Serving opportunities could be:

- Room setup/breakdown
- Special events organizer
- Building projects team

Task Structured

You tend to:

- Get the job done
- Focus on results
- Follow an agenda
- Appreciate clear direction

Serving opportunities could be:

- Sound and lighting team
- Offering taker/counter
- Drama set builder

People Unstructured

You tend to:

- Be very conversational
- Be flexible
- Relate well with others
- Like spontaneous situations

Serving opportunities could be:

- Crisis hotline
- Greeter team
- Information center

People Structured

You tend to:

- Project warmth
- Like defined relationships
- Relate well with others
- Enjoy familiar surroundings

Serving opportunities could be:

- Small group leader
- Membership team
- Assimilation strategies

COMFORT ZONES

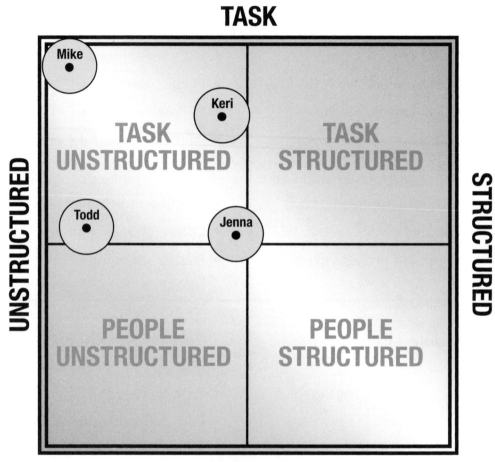

TASK

UNSTRUCTURED   **STRUCTURED**

TASK UNSTRUCTURED

TASK STRUCTURED

PEOPLE UNSTRUCTURED

PEOPLE STRUCTURED

PEOPLE

Mike
Keri
Todd
Jenna

Your Comfort Zone   ● **Where You Are**

Your Comfort Zone is a condition of ease and well-being.

PERSONAL STYLE SUMMARY

A. _____

B. _____

Know what your Personal Style preferences are
. . . and express them whenever possible!

SERVANT PROFILE: MINISTRY PASSION

God cares for every need.

God chose to take a piece of his *heart* — and put it into your heart—in the form of a Ministry Passion.

MINISTRY PASSION

Ministry Passion is a heartfelt desire that compels us to make a difference for the kingdom of God.

Our Passion may . . .

  Right a wrong

  Meet a need

  Solve a problem

  Serve a cause

  Change a life

Three truths about Ministry Passion:

1. Ministry Passion is God-given.

2. There is no right or wrong Ministry Passion. Ministry Passions are just different.

3. Ministry Passion answers the " WHERE " question: "Where do I serve?"

God has a passion for us . . .

For God so loved the world that he gave his one and only Son . . .

John 3:16

God also has a purpose for the passion he puts in our hearts . . .

For it is God who works in you to will and to act according to his good purpose.

Philippians 2:13

The psalmist puts it this way . . .

> *Trust in the Lord and do good; dwell in the land and enjoy safe pasture. Delight yourself in the* LORD *and* **he will give you the desires of your heart.**
>
> Psalm 37:3–4

Jesus himself promises . . .

> *If you remain in me and my words remain in you, ask whatever you wish, and it will be given you.*
>
> John 15:7

The apostle Paul had a God-given Ministry Passion to preach to the Gentiles (Galatians 1:15–16).

Other words you might use to communicate your Ministry Passion are:

KEY WORDS FOR MINISTRY PASSION		
anger	assignment	burden
call	compassion	destiny
dream	energy	God's will
impact	inspired	legacy
motivated	passion	purpose
significance	vision	

Remember ... Ministry Passions are NOT Spiritual Gifts.

Spiritual Gifts are functions or tasks you perform.

Ministry Passions are feelings or desires that ___MOTIVATE___ you to serve in a particular ministry.

MINISTRY PASSION ASSESSMENT

The purpose of this assessment is to assist you in the identification and articulation of your God-given Ministry Passion. The results will release greater motivation and enthusiasm in your life and ministry.

Directions

1. You may not be able to answer all of the questions. That is okay. The Assessment is designed to explore a variety of ways God speaks to us about our Ministry Passion. He has probably spoken to you in some of these ways, but not all of them.

2. Prayerfully consider your responses to each question.

3. Since this is an individual exercise, complete the Assessment on your own. (You can talk about it with others afterward.)

4. There are no right or wrong answers. You have permission to say what is on your heart.

5. At this point, do not consider *whether* you could do it or *how* you could do it. All you need to do right now is *name* it.

6. Assume there are no obstacles to hinder you from fulfilling your heart's desire (Ministry Passion). Assume everything is taken care of ... family, money, career, time, etc.

MINISTRY PASSION ASSESSMENT

1. If you could snap your fingers and know that you wouldn't fail, what would you do for others?

   _____

   _____

2. What do you repeatedly see that annoys or angers you, which if changed, would be more glorifying to God and edifying to others?

   _____

   _____

3. I care about some things more than other things. I care most about . . .

   _____

   _____

4. At the end of my life, I'd love to be able to look back and know I'd done something about . . .

   _____

   _____

5. Use the chart on the following page to help uncover a theme in your life that may give you an insight into your Ministry Passion.

List your top five to seven most meaningful and positive life experiences. Briefly describe what you achieved and why it meant so much to *you*.

> NOTE: *Your experiences may have taken place at home, work, school, or during your free time. It may have been a clock you fixed or a dress you made. It may have been a puzzle you put together or an award you received. It may have been helping some friends move, building a house, winning an election, or giving to someone in need. Remember, list the experiences that you enjoyed doing and left you feeling fulfilled.*

	Positive Experiences	Why is this experience meaningful to me?	Theme Identified
A			
B			
C			
D			
E			
F			
G			

Looking over your responses to questions 1 through 5, what theme(s) or patterns seem to be most evident and repeating?

Reoccurring Theme(s) . . .

- _____

  _____

- _____

  _____

6. Some Ministry Passions can be centered around a people group or a social issue. Consider these partial lists and indicate any that tug at your heart. It is *okay* if you do not have a desire to make a difference in any of these areas.

People Groups:

Infants	Children	Youth
Teen moms	Single parents	College students
Divorced	Widowed	Singles
Career women	Young marrieds	Refugees
Parents	Empty nesters	Homeless
Unemployed	Elderly	Disabled
Prisoners	Poor	Hospitalized
_____	_____	_____

Social Issues:

Environment	Child care	Homosexuality
Discipleship	AIDS	Politics
Violence	Injustice	Racism
Education	Addictions	Economic
Reaching the lost	Technology	Health care
Poverty	Family	Abortion
Hunger	Literacy	Nutrition
_____	_____	_____

7. Based on your responses to this assessment, which ONE of these Ministry Passion Categories best reflects your area of passion?

CHECK HERE	PASSION CATEGORIES	DESCRIPTION
	Celebration Ministries	*The heart of these ministries is directed toward God by engaging the church in the Word, worship, song, the arts, etc.*
	Outreach Ministries	*The heart of these ministries is focused on relating, reaching, and connecting unbelievers and the unchurched to a relationship with Christ and his church.*
	Connecting Ministries	*The heart of these ministries is assimilating visitors, attenders, and members into a relationship with Christ and the church through hospitality, fellowship, belonging, and encouragement.*
	Equipping Ministries	*The heart of these ministries is maturing believers in the area of their gifts, ministry, training, and leadership. It serves a variety of life-stage and affinity-based groups for growth, accountability, and service.*
	Caring Ministries	*The heart of these ministries is assisting people in the church and community with their physical, emotional, relational, and spiritual health through the grace, love, and resources of the kingdom.*
	Supporting Ministries	*The heart of these ministries is freeing other people, leaders, and ministries from practical concerns to keep focused on their ministry goals. They involve structuring the systems and procedures to serve and support people and ministries.*

SUMMARY

8. At this time, I would say . . .

My Ministry Passion is to . . . or for . . .

My Ministry Passion Category is:

DVD: CLARIFYING YOUR MINISTRY PASSION

Directions

Watch how Lauren clarifies her Ministry Passion. Keep in mind the questions below.

1. How did Lauren first describe her passion?

2. After her first ministry experience, what did she realize and how did it make her feel?

3. While talking with the director of small groups, what did Lauren come to better understand about her Ministry Passion?

4. What additional insights came to Lauren, months later, which helped her better understand her Ministry Passion? (The conversation in the coffee shop with a member of her small group, Christina, and a couple of fellow small group leaders)

"The Promise of Ministry"

Let us throw off everything that hinders and the sin that so easily entangles, and let us run with perseverance the race marked out for us.

Hebrews 12:1

For we are God's workmanship, created in Christ Jesus to do good works, which God prepared in advance for us to do.

Ephesians 2:10

GROUPS: CLARIFYING YOUR MINISTRY PASSION

Directions

1. Write your Ministry Passion in the space provided on the next page.

2. Form a group with two or three other people.

3. Share your Ministry Passion and why you feel as you do about it.

4. Then listen and respond as the group asks you questions about your Passion.

5. Use the space provided below to write down additional words, phrases, or insights that help you better understand and further clarify your Ministry Passion.

Write your Ministry Passion here (from page 129):

I have a passion to / for . . .

Write additional words, phrases, or insights from the group:

Would you state your passion any differently in light of the group's comments and questions? If so, rewrite your Ministry Passion here:

I have a passion to . . . for:

_____

_____

Passion Category: (see page 128)

_____

_____

POSSIBLE HINDRANCES

Your Ministry Passion can be hindered, confused or even distorted by:

- Low self-esteem

- Pride

- Unrepentant sin

Some people are afraid to name their Ministry Passion because they have a fear of:

- Rejection

- Accountability

- Failure

- Success

God has given you a Ministry Passion as a part of your life purpose.

> *Let us throw off everything that hinders and the sin that so easily entangles, and let us run with perseverance the race marked out for us.*
>
> Hebrews 12:1

> *For we are God's workmanship, created in Christ Jesus to do good works, which God prepared in advance for us to do.*
>
> Ephesians 2:10

YOUR *SERVANT PROFILE*

The *Servant Profile* links together your:

- Spiritual Gifts

- Personal Style

- Ministry Passion

Remember, you can have ...

Any Spiritual Gift, with

Any Personal Style, with

Any Ministry Passion!

Directions

1. On the following page, write in your top three Spiritual Gifts as you best understand them (from page 68).

2. Write in your Personal Style (from page 111).

3. Write in your Ministry Passion (from page 133). If you are still clarifying it, then write down your Ministry Passion Category from page 129.

YOUR *SERVANT PROFILE*

SPIRITUAL GIFTS

1. _____

2. _____

3. _____

PERSONAL STYLE

_____

MINISTRY PASSION

Passion Category _____

EXAMPLES:

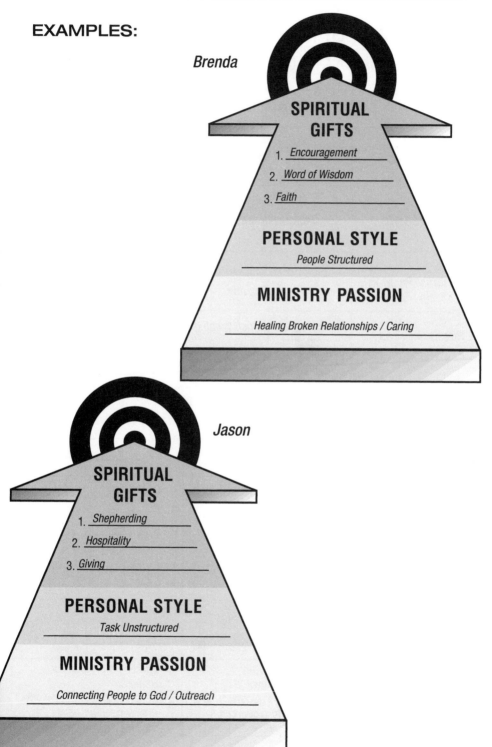

Brenda

SPIRITUAL GIFTS

1. Encouragement
2. Word of Wisdom
3. Faith

PERSONAL STYLE

People Structured

MINISTRY PASSION

Healing Broken Relationships / Caring

Jason

SPIRITUAL GIFTS

1. Shepherding
2. Hospitality
3. Giving

PERSONAL STYLE

Task Unstructured

MINISTRY PASSION

Connecting People to God / Outreach

Examples of Ministry Possibilities

Situation 1: SAME Gift ... DIFFERENT Passions

	DARON	WENDY
Spiritual Gifts	1. Teaching	1. Teaching
Personal Style	Task Unstructured	People Structured
Ministry Passion	Fellowship Ministries/ Senior Citizens	Discipleship Ministries/ Discipleship
Possible Areas of Service	• Writing self-guided training programs • Leading Bible studies in retirement homes	• Leading a small group • Mentoring • Teach new believer classes

Situation 2: SAME Passion ... DIFFERENT Gifts

	RYAN	MELINDA
Spiritual Gifts	1. Administration 2. Helps	1. Giving 2. Hospitality
Personal Style	People Structured	Task Unstructured
Ministry Passion	Caring Ministries/Children with Difficult Life Situations	Caring Ministries/Children with Difficult Life Situations
Possible Areas of Service	• Organizing events to serve children of divorce • Identifying and attracting people and resources to meet the need	• Funding a program or materials • Supporting volunteer workers by opening her home for meetings and prayer

Identifying your place of service is more of an *art* than it is a *science.*

When you can serve and faithfully express your *Servant Profile* (Gifts, Style, Passion), it is a good

" MINISTRY FIT ."

GROUPS: YOUR MINISTRY POSSIBILITIES

Directions

1. Write down your *Servant Profile* information on page 141.

2. Form a group with two or three others.

3. Decide who will go first in your group. They will share their *Servant Profile* with the group. As you listen, write down their name, Gifts, Style, and Passion in one of the blank Profiles provided on page 142. When it's your turn, use the Profile on page 141.

4. Focus on that person, who remains silent, while the others look at his or her *Servant Profile* and suggest Ministry Possibilities that reflect their God-given Gifts, Style, and Passion.

5. As you are listing possibilities, do not be limited to positions or ministries that you already know about, but imagine what would be possible for them to do if such a ministry or position did exist. Do not be limited to the ministries your church, denomination, or community may or may not have. God just might want to create something new!

6. After 4 minutes, the next person shares their Profile and the group lists Ministry Possibilities for them. Each person should have a 4-minute rotation.

NOTE: Come up with as many serving ideas as possible. Do not take group time to debate or talk too long about a suggestion.

SPIRITUAL GIFTS

1. _____

2. _____

3. _____

PERSONAL STYLE

_____

MINISTRY PASSION

Passion Category _____

Your Profile from p. 136

Some of Your Ministry Possibilities:

1. _____   6. _____

2. _____   7. _____

3. _____   8. _____

4. _____   9. _____

5. _____   10. _____

Look over the suggestions that were given to you as Ministry Possibilities. Circle the two or three that interest you the most.

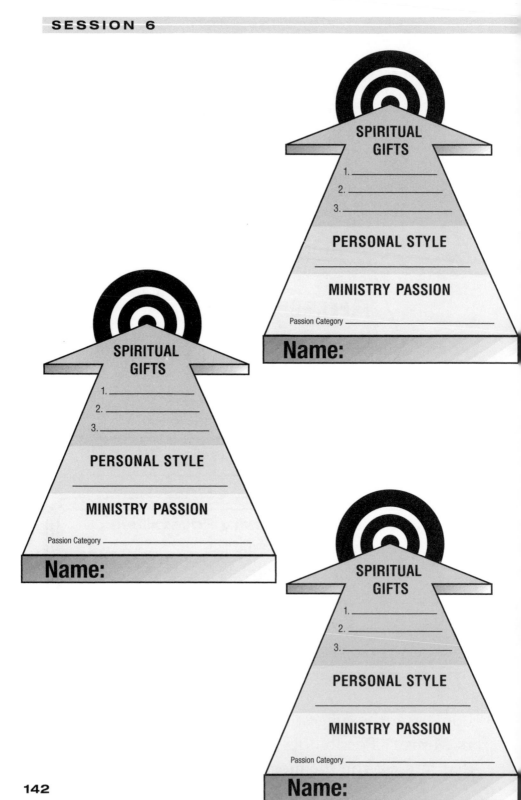

SPIRITUAL GIFTS

1. _____
2. _____
3. _____

PERSONAL STYLE

_____

MINISTRY PASSION

Passion Category _____

Name:

SPIRITUAL GIFTS

1. _____
2. _____
3. _____

PERSONAL STYLE

_____

MINISTRY PASSION

Passion Category _____

Name:

SPIRITUAL GIFTS

1. _____
2. _____
3. _____

PERSONAL STYLE

_____

MINISTRY PASSION

Passion Category _____

Name:

Factors that impact your Next Step:

- Time Availability
- Spiritual Maturity

Availability and Maturity determine whether you should make your:

- Unique Contribution
- Community Contribution

Unique Contribution

- Serving where you are able to reflect your *Servant Profile*

Community Contribution

- Serving where you aren't able to reflect your *Servant Profile*
- Serving in general ways

A Lifetime of Service

Believers are to be worshipers for a lifetime
(John 4:20–24)
> ... not just weekend worshipers with
> summers off.

Believers are to be stewards for a lifetime
(Matthew 25:14–30)
> ... not just token givers tipping God.

Believers are to be servants for a lifetime
(1 Peter 4:10; Romans 12:1)
> ... not just seasonal servants taking turns
> and rotating out.

Worship, Stewardship, and Servanthood apply to
every believer:
> ... young and old
> ... single and married
> ... educated and uneducated
> ... working and unemployed
> ... male and female

Serving is for a lifetime ... for __EVERY__
believer!

CIRCLE OF GIFTS

What have you identified as your top Spiritual Gift?

- Administration
- Apostleship
- Craftsmanship
- Creative
  Communication
- Discernment
- Encouragement
- Evangelism
- Faith

- Giving
- Healing
- Helps
- Hospitality
- Intercession
- Interpretation
- Knowledge
- Leadership
- Mercy

- Miracles
- Prophecy
- Shepherding
- Teaching
- Tongues
- Wisdom
- Any other
   Spiritual Gifts . . .

God only holds us accountable for the Spiritual
Gifts he has given us!

How to Maximize Your Coaching Experience

Your Coach will assist you in taking the next step in your journey to fruitful and fulfilling service. Be sure to sign up for a time that is good for you and your Coach as soon as possible.

1. Before You Meet with Your Coach

   - Pray for wisdom and discernment for both you and your Coach.

   - Review your *Servant Profile*, and be prepared to discuss your Spiritual Gifts, Personal Style, and Ministry Passion with your Coach.

   - Reflect on the information regarding your Time Availability and Spiritual Maturity (pages 149–50).

   - Complete your *Personal Resources Survey*, if you have not already done so (pages 164–67).

   - Identify three to five possible ministries you feel reflect your *Servant Profile* and you are interested in.

- Together, you and your Coach will discuss them and consider which one(s) would be best to pursue at this time.

2. If for any reason you are unable to keep your scheduled appointment, please call them as far in advance as you can. Your thoughtfulness is greatly appreciated.

3. After meeting with a Coach, contact the specific ministries you identified for possible involvement within ten days, while the ideas and descriptions are still fresh.

4. Continue in prayer as you are devoting time, reflection, and exploration concerning your involvement in a serving position.

5. If you have any questions, call your Coach. They are there to serve you through the process. It is their ministry!

Time Availability and Spiritual Maturity

TIME AVAILABILITY

Our season or stage in life may affect our availability.

- *Do you have young children?*
- *Are you married?*
- *Single?*
- *Single with children?*
- *How much do you travel for work?*
- *How far do you live from the place of potential ministry?*
- *What community activities are you involved with?*
- *Etc.*

We support a balanced life . . . and that includes serving the Lord!

After assessing current time commitments and priorities, do you have the time to begin making your unique contribution? Will you *make* the time? If you can't, you could still find a related position to better fit your schedule and serve making a community contribution (see page 143).

Using the chart on the next page, place a *check* indicating the amount of time you are making available and committing to serve according to your *Servant Profile*.

CHECK HERE	TIME AVAILABILITY	DESCRIPTION
	Unavailable	Cannot serve at this time. I am not sure where or how I could serve with my time.
	Limited	1–2 hours per week
	Moderate	2–4 hours per week
	Expanding	4 or more hours per week

SPIRITUAL MATURITY

Take a spiritual "snapshot" of your relationship with Christ. Using the chart below, place a check indicating how you would characterize your current level of Spiritual Maturity.

CHECK HERE	SPIRITUAL MATURITY	DESCRIPTION
	Seeker/Unsure	I am not sure how to describe my current level of Spiritual Maturity. (Discuss with Coach)
	New/Young	I have recently become a Christian, or I have been a Christian for some time and recently am understanding what it means to have a personal relationship with Jesus Christ.
	Stable/Growing	I am regular in worship, fellowship, giving, and pursuing a life of greater devotion to Christ. I am teachable and sensitive to the leading of the Holy Spirit in my life.
	Modeling/Guiding	I am a fully devoted follower of Jesus Christ. I have reached a level of Spiritual Maturity and confidence in my walk with God that others look to me as an example of faithfulness.

My Ministry Plan . . . "Next Steps"

Following this course, I will do the following:

❏ Schedule an appointment and meet with my Network Coach.

By when?_____

❏ Pray over the church's list of ministry opportunities and identify the three that interest me most.

By when?_____

❏ Contact ministry leaders to discuss the serving opportunities which will best reflect my *Servant Profile.*

By when?_____

❏ Commit to serving in a ministry.

By when?_____

❏ I need to:_____

By when?_____

❏ I need to:_____

By when?_____

Created and called to glorify God and edify others!

Spiritual Gifts
Are NOT . . .

1. Natural Talents
(cooking, sports, etc.)

NATURAL TALENTS	SPIRITUAL GIFTS
Given at physical birth	*Given at spiritual birth*
God-given to all people	*God-given to believers*

Sometimes a talent can be transformed by the Holy Spirit:

Manager ›››➡ into ›››➡ Leadership/Administration
Salesperson ›››➡ into ›››➡ Evangelism
Singer ›››➡ into ›››➡ Creative Communication
Carpenter ›››➡ into ›››➡ Craftsmanship

Both natural talents and spiritual gifts need to be identified and developed.

2. The fruit of the Spirit
(love, joy, peace, etc., Galatians 5:22–23)

FRUIT OF THE SPIRIT	SPIRITUAL GIFTS
"Being" Qualities	*"Doing" Qualities*
Attitudes	*Aptitudes*
By-product of healthy walk with God	*Supernatural abilities given by the Holy Spirit*
Necessary for effective ministry	*Necessary for effective ministry*

3. Church positions
(pastor, Sunday school teacher, etc.)

MINISTRY POSITION/TITLE	SPIRITUAL GIFTS
Pastor	*Teaching, Apostleship, Leadership, Shepherding*
Sunday School Teacher	*Encouragement, Hospitality, Shepherding, Teaching*
Church Leader	*Apostleship, Evangelist, Shepherding, Leadership*

4. Christian Disciplines
(fasting, meditation, study, tithing, etc.)

CHRISTIAN DISCIPLINE	SPIRITUAL GIFTS
All should be practiced in a believer's life	*A few will be practiced in a believer's life*
Builds up the individual believer	*Builds up the body of Christ ... the church*
Everyone should exercise all the disciplines	*Everyone should express their Spiritual Gift*

A Sample List of Ministry Passions

1. Abortion
2. Abused Women
3. Addictions Recovery
4. AIDS
5. Animals
6. Beauty and Order
7. Building Esteem
8. Career Women
9. Child Care
10. Children
11. Children in Need
12. Church
13. Church Effectiveness
14. Church Renewal
15. College Students
16. Connecting People
17. Crisis Intervention
18. Disabled
19. Discipleship
20. Divorced
21. Economic
22. Education
23. Elderly
24. Empty Nesters
25. Environment
26. Family
27. Fellowship
28. Relational Harmony
29. Health Care
30. Help Hurting Adults
31. Helping the Helpless
32. Homeless
33. Homosexuality
34. Hospice Care
35. Hospitalized
36. Hunger
37. Immature Believers
38. Infants
39. Injustice
40. International Ministry
41. Leadership Development
42. Literacy
43. Making Systems Work and Serving People
44. Mentoring
45. Missions
46. Parents
47. Politics
48. Poor
49. Poverty
50. Prisoners
51. Racism
52. Reaching the Lost
53. Refugees
54. Single Parents
55. Singles
56. Spiritual Warfare
57. Technology
58. Teen Moms
59. Unemployed
60. Violence
61. Widowed
62. Young Marrieds
63. Youth

Passion without action . . . is merely a dream.

Action without passion . . . passes the time.

Passion with action . . . can change the world!

(Author Unknown)

Resources

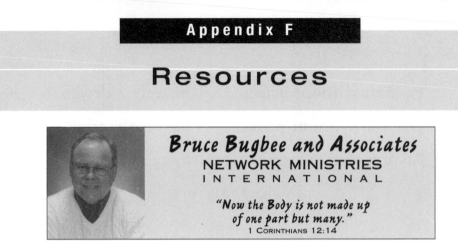

Bruce Bugbee and Associates
NETWORK MINISTRIES
I N T E R N A T I O N A L

*"Now the Body is not made up
of one part but many."*
1 CORINTHIANS 12:14

Bruce Bugbee has been actively involved with gift-based ministries since 1970. He has provided vision and leadership for churches and individuals seeking to better understand who God has made them to be and how they can make a difference in a meaningful place of service.

In 1986, Bruce coauthored Network with Don Cousins and Bill Hybels. It has helped volunteers discover their God-given Spiritual Gifts, Ministry Passions, Personal Style, spiritual maturity, and availability for their rightful place and purpose in the body of Christ through the local church.

Network Ministries International was established in 1993 to serve and support the ministry and mission of the local church in the effective and efficient use of God's people for kingdom purposes. Building up believers, equipping leaders, and establishing harmonious systems mark the impact of Network Ministries International.

Following is a partial list of materials from Network Ministries International to assist you in the identification, placement, and equipping of enthusiastic and gifted servers in your church. Visit our website at:

www.networkministries.com
or contact our offices directly at (800) 588-8833
Church discounts available

- Network Ministry Materials

  Network Kit (includes the following . . . and each is available separately)

  Leader's Guide

  Participant's Guide

  DVD with 6 teaching vignettes, vision casting, and coach training

  CD with PowerPoint™ Presentation, Coach's Guide, and User's Guide

- *What You Do Best in the Body of Christ, Revised and Expanded*

  This new edition includes questions for reflection at the end of each chapter and assessments for your Spiritual Gifts, Personal Style, and Ministry Passion. Ideal for small groups, Sunday school, and individuals. Great resource for new members. Give your leadership teams a vision for the Network process.

- *Discover Your Spiritual Gifts the Network Way!* (NEW)

  Now you can discover your Spiritual Gifts with the best resources available. Includes four gift assessments (experiences, traits, convictions, and observations) plus a ministry assessment!

- *The Gift Book*

  This resource contains an in-depth study of each of the Spiritual Gifts. Once you have identified your gift, you can now study and learn how to develop it. (Available late 2005)

- *Leadership C.A.R.E.™*

  Equipping churches require equippers! Walk your ministry leaders through the process from being primarily program planners and event coordinators to leading gift-based ministry teams as people equippers.

  Includes Leader's Guide with PowerPoint™ Ministry Workbook

- The Network Center*online*™ Database

  A database for volunteer placement and ministry management. Keep in touch will all your people resources through the "net"—the Network Center*online* database. A ready-to-use people-flow tracking system that helps you keep track of all the Spiritual Gifts, Styles, and Ministry Passions of your servers. Store and sort through all your Ministry Position Descriptions too! Try it free on the Demo Site:

  www.networkcenteronline.com
  (ID=9   Password=serve)

- Leadership Retreats and Onsite Training

  Bring the vision and expertise you need to your church. Bruce Bugbee will work with your staff, church leaders, and congregation. Schedule an event, retreat, or consultation. He brings biblical teaching, passion for the church, leadership understanding, and practical truth with humor and over thirty years of gift-based ministry experience.

Contact Bruce Bugbee at

Network Ministries International

for

vision casting...ministry implementation...equipping leaders

staff@brucebugbee.com

www.networkministries.com   800.588.8833

Church Discounts Available!

Network Course Evaluation

1. How would you rate this course overall?

1	2	3	4	5
Poor				Excellent

2. Which aspects of the course were most meaningful?

_____

_____

_____

3. Which aspects of the course were least useful?

_____

_____

_____

4. What, if anything, would you like to see included or changed?

_____

_____

_____

5. To what extent did this course meet your expectations in terms of value and quality?

1	2	3	4	5
Less Than Expected		Met Expectations		Went Beyond Expectatio

6. Circle the session numbers you attended or completed.

Session: 1   2   3   4   5   6

7. Check the assessments you completed.

Spiritual Gifts:

❏ *Experience Assessment* (pages 53–64)

❏ *Observations Assessments* (pages 65–67)

❏ *Reference Assessment* (pages 72–95)

❏ *Personal Style Assessment* (pages 107–111)

❏ *Ministry Passion Assessment* (pages 124–129)

8. Would you recommend others attend this course?

1	2	3	4	5
Definitely would not				Definitely would

9. Comments or Questions:

_____

_____

_____

_____

_____

_____

Personal Resources Survey

PERSONAL

Name _____ Network Sessions Month/Year _____

Address _____ Apt#_____

City_____ State_____ Zip _____

Home Phone _____ _____ Work Phone (_____) _____

Birth Date _____ ❏ Male   ❏ Female

FAMILY

Marital Status: ❏ Single   ❏ Married

Spouse's Name: _____ Birth Date: _____

Children's Names:

_____ ❏ M   ❏ F   Birth Date:_____
_____ ❏ M   ❏ F   Birth Date:_____
_____ ❏ M   ❏ F   Birth Date:_____
_____ ❏ M   ❏ F   Birth Date:_____
_____ ❏ M   ❏ F   Birth Date:_____
_____ ❏ M   ❏ F   Birth Date:_____

CHURCH

When did you start attending the church? Month/Year: _____

Are you a member?   ❏ Yes   ❏ No

Small Groups: ❏ I am in one (Leader's name) _____
                     ❏ I would like to be in one
                     ❏ I used to be in one (Leader's name) _____
                     ❏ Other: _____

CURRENT MINISTRY INVOLVEMENT

Which of the following ministries are you now involved in?   ❏ None

Ministry _____ Leader_____

Ministry _____ Leader_____

List other ministries or community groups outside the church in which you are involved:

Ministry/Group _____

Ministry/Group _____

PAST MINISTRY INVOLVEMENT

Which of the following ministries have you been involved in in the past?   ❏ None

Ministry _____ Leader_____

Ministry _____ Leader_____

List other ministries or community groups outside the church in which you have been involved:

Ministry/Group _____

Ministry/Group _____

PERSONAL RESOURCES SURVEY—2

SERVANT PROFILE AND COACHING SUMMARY

Complete Prior to Meeting with Your Coach

My **Spiritual Gifts** are:
1. _____
2. _____
3. _____

Passion Category:
1. _____
2. _____

I have a **Passion** for:
1. _____
2. _____

Shaded Area to Be Completed by Coach

My **Spiritual Gifts** are:
1. _____
2. _____
3. _____

Passion Category:
1. _____
2. _____

I have a **Passion** for:
1. _____
2. _____

My **Personal Style** is:
❏ People/Structured   ❏ People/Unstructured
❏ Task/Structured   ❏ Task/Unstructured

I would describe my **spiritual maturity** as:
❏ Seeker/Unsure   ❏ New/Young Believer
❏ Stable/Growing Believer   ❏ Leading/Guiding Believer

I would describe my current **availability** as:
❏ Limited, 1–2 hrs   ❏ Moderate, 2–4 hrs
❏ Significant, 4+ hrs   ❏ Not sure

I would like to know more about the following ministries:

_____

_____

_____

The following ministries were identified as possible places of service: M-Category: _____

A. _____   B. _____   C. _____

Coach: _____   Phone: _____

Comments: _____

_____

PERSONAL RESOURCES SURVEY—3

EMPLOYMENT

❏ I am employed   ❏ Self-Employed   ❏ Unemployed

Name of Company _____

Title/Responsibilities _____

Product or Service _____

EDUCATION

❏ High School   ❏ Some College   ❏ Other
❏ College   ❏ Master's Degree
❏ Doctorate   ❏ Professional Degree

SPIRITUAL JOURNEY

How did you come to know Christ personally? How do you maintain your relationship?

_____
_____
_____
_____
_____
_____
_____
_____
_____
_____
_____
_____
_____
_____
_____
_____
_____
_____
_____
_____

PERSONAL RESOURCES SURVEY—4

In addition to your *Servant Profile*, please go through each area, carefully marking the boxes which indicate talents or skills in which you have proven ability. In other words, indicate areas in which you have demonstrated a reasonable amount of confidence and competence. You are not making a commitment to serve in any area where you check a box, but we would like to have this information on file in case of special needs. Be honest and fair in your self-evaluation.

Professional Services

- ❏ Mental Health
- ❏ Social Work
- ❏ Financial
- ❏ Dental
- ❏ Medical
- ❏ Chiropractic
- ❏ Legal
- ❏ Accounting
- ❏ Bookkeeping
- ❏ Taxes
- ❏ Nursing
- ❏ Landscaping
- ❏ Carpet Cleaning
- ❏ Window Washing
- ❏ Engineer
- ❏ Lifeguard
- ❏ Counseling
- ❏ Career Counseling
- ❏ Unemployment
- ❏ Day Care Director
- ❏ Law Enforcement
- ❏ Personnel Mgr.
- ❏ Public Relations
- ❏ Advertising
- ❏ Television:_____
- ❏ Radio
- ❏ Computer Prog.
- ❏ Paramedic/EMT
- ❏ Systems Analyst
- ❏ Journalist/Writer
- ❏ _____

Art

- ❏ Layout
- ❏ Photography
- ❏ Graphics
- ❏ Multimedia
- ❏ Mailers
- ❏ Crafts
- ❏ Artist
- ❏ Banners
- ❏ Decorating
- ❏ _____

Teaching or Assisting

- ❏ Preschool
- ❏ Elementary
- ❏ Junior High
- ❏ Senior High
- ❏ Single Adults (18–29)
- ❏ Single Adults (30+)
- ❏ Couples
- ❏ Men's Group
- ❏ Women's Group
- ❏ Tutoring
- ❏ Learning Disabled
- ❏ Researcher
- ❏ Aerobics
- ❏ Budget Counselor
- ❏ _____

Mechanical

- ❏ Copier Repair
- ❏ Diesel Mechanic
- ❏ Auto Mechanic
- ❏ Small Engine Repair
- ❏ Mower Repair
- ❏ Machinist
- ❏ _____

Office Skills

- ❏ Computers
- ❏ Word Processing
- ❏ Receptionist
- ❏ Office Manager
- ❏ Data Entry
- ❏ Filing
- ❏ Mail Room
- ❏ Library
- ❏ Transcription
- ❏ Shorthand
- ❏ _____

Missions

- ❏ Long Term
- ❏ Short Term
- ❏ Missionary
- ❏ Evangelism
- ❏ _____

Theatrical

- ❏ Actor/Actress
- ❏ Poet
- ❏ Dance
- ❏ Mime
- ❏ Puppets
- ❏ Clowning
- ❏ Audio Production
- ❏ Sound/Mixing
- ❏ Lighting
- ❏ Set Construction
- ❏ Set Design
- ❏ Stagehand
- ❏ Scriptwriter
- ❏ _____

Construction

- ❏ General Contractor
- ❏ Architect
- ❏ Carpenter: General
- ❏ Carpenter: Finish
- ❏ Carpenter: Cabinet
- ❏ Electrician
- ❏ Plumbing
- ❏ Heating
- ❏ Air-conditioning
- ❏ Painting
- ❏ Papering
- ❏ Masonry
- ❏ Roofing
- ❏ Telephones
- ❏ Drywall Finishing
- ❏ Concrete
- ❏ Carpet Installer
- ❏ Interior Design
- ❏ Drafting
- ❏ _____

Working With

- ❏ Handicapped
- ❏ Hearing Impaired (Signing)
- ❏ Incarcerated
- ❏ Learning Disabilities
- ❏ Nursing Homes/Shut-Ins
- ❏ Hospital Visitation
- ❏ Meals on Wheels
- ❏ Housing for Homeless
- ❏ _____

General Help

- ❏ Cashier
- ❏ Child Care
- ❏ Customer Service
- ❏ Food Service
- ❏ Gardening
- ❏ Building Maintenance
- ❏ Grounds Maintenance
- ❏ Transportation
- ❏ Snow Removal
- ❏ Catering/Cooking
- ❏ Weddings
- ❏ Bookstore
- ❏ Tape Duplication
- ❏ Plant Care (Indoor)
- ❏ Sports Official
- ❏ Sports Instructor
- ❏ Website Development
- ❏ Website Maintenance
- ❏ _____

Musical

- ❏ Choir Director
- ❏ Choir
- ❏ Soloist
- ❏ Instrument
- ❏ Composer
- ❏ Arranger
- ❏ Piano Tuner
- ❏ _____

Are there any other products, specific resources, skills, interests, talents, abilities, or unique opportunities (example: permitted access to specialized purchasing/discounts for the church) that you would like to offer to the church?_____

I understand that this information will be made available only to responsible and appropriate staff and ministry leaders at this church.

Signature: _____ Date: _____

Observation Assessments

On the following pages you will find three identical *Observation Assessments*. Remove them and give an *Observation Assessment* to three people.

For complete directions, see page 65.

Spiritual Gifts Discovery

I'd like your opinion!

I am seeking to better understand how God has equipped me to serve others. One part of the process involves getting feedback from a few people who know me reasonably well. Your thoughts about what I do best and the way I relate to others will be very helpful. Please take a few minutes to complete this assessment.

My name is:_____

These are my observations of:

_____

Directions:

1. Please read the descriptions below.

2. Mark each one according to how true it is of the person you are describing.

3. Place your score to each statement in the appropriately numbered box on the answer sheet on pages 2–5. Respond by using the following scale:

SCORE   MEANING
- 3 = Consistently/Definitely True
- 2 = Most of the Time/Usually True
- 1 = Some of the Time/Once in a While
- 0 = Don't Know/Haven't Observed

1

IMPORTANT:

- Answer according to what seems to be true of them most of the time ... not what you would like them to be, or think they should be.

- To what degree do these statements reflect their tendencies?

- Return the assessment as soon as you have completed it. Thanks!

Observation Assessment #1

		Consistently– Definitely True	Most of the Time– Usually True	Some of the Time– Once in a While	Don't Know– Haven't Observed
A	Develops strategies or plans to reach identified goals; organizes people, tasks, and events; helps organizations or groups become more efficient; creates order out of organizational chaos.	3	2	1	0
B	Works creatively with wood, cloth, metal, paints, glass, etc.; works with different kinds of tools; makes things for practical uses; designs and builds things; works with his or her hands.	3	2	1	0
C	Communicates with variety and creativity; develops and uses particular artistic skills (art, drama, music, photography, etc.); finds new and fresh ways to communicate ideas to others.	3	2	1	0
D	Strengthens and reassures troubled people; encourages or challenges them; motivates others to grow; supports those who seem to be stuck and need to take action.	3	2	1	0
E	Trusts God to answer prayer and encourages others to do the same; has confidence in God's continuing presence and ability to help, even in difficult times; moves forward in spite of difficulties or opposition.	3	2	1	0

2

Observation Assessment #1

		Consistently– Definitely True	Most of the Time– Usually True	Some of the Time– Once in a While	Don't Know– Haven't Observed	
F	Gives liberally and joyfully to people in financial need; gives generously to projects requiring substantial support; manages his or her money well in order to free more of it for other people and causes.	3	2	1	0	
G	Works behind the scenes to support the work of others; finds small things that need to be done and does them without being asked; helps wherever needed, even with routine or mundane tasks.	3	2	1	0	
H	Meets new people and helps them to feel welcome; entertains guests; opens his or her home to others who need a safe, supportive environment; puts people at ease in unfamiliar surroundings.	3	2	1	0	
I	Continually offers to pray for others; has confidence in the Lord's protection; spends a lot of time praying; is convinced that God moves in direct response to prayer.	3	2	1	0	
J	Takes responsibility for directing groups; motivates and guides others to reach important goals; manages people and resources well; influences others to perform to the best of their abilities.	3	2	1	0	
K	Empathizes with hurting people; patiently and compassionately walks with people through painful experiences; helps those generally regarded as undeserving or beyond help.	3	2	1	0	
L	Pioneers new undertakings (such as a new church or ministry); serves in another country or community; adapts to different cultures and surroundings; demonstrates cultural awareness and sensitivity.	3	2	1	0	
M	Speaks with conviction to bring change in the lives of others; exposes cultural trends, teaching, or events that are morally wrong or harmful; boldly speaks truth even in places where it may be unpopular.	3	2	1	0	

3

Observation Assessment #1

		Consistently– Definitely True	Most of the Time– Usually True	Some of the Time– Once in a While	Don't Know– Haven't Observed	
N	*Looks for opportunities to build relationships with unbelievers; communicates openly and effectively about his or her faith; talks about spiritual matters with those who don't believe.*	3	2	1	0	
O	*Faithfully provides long-term support and nurture for a group of people; provides guidance for the whole person; patiently but firmly nurtures others in their development as believers.*	3	2	1	0	
P	*Studies, understands, and communicates biblical truth; develops appropriate teaching material and presents it effectively; communicates in ways that motivate others to change.*	3	2	1	0	
Q	*Distinguishes between truth and error, good and evil; accurately judges character; sees through phoniness and deceit; helps others to see rightness or wrongness in life situations.*	3	2	1	0	
R	*Carefully studies and researches subjects he or she wants to understand better; shares his or her knowledge and insights with others when asked; sometimes gains information that is not attained by natural observation or means.*	3	2	1	0	
S	*Sees simple, practical solutions in the midst of conflict or confusion; gives helpful advice to others facing complicated life situations; helps people take practical action to solve real problems.*	3	2	1	0	
T	*Demonstrates the power of God by bringing restoration to the sick and diseased by laying hands on them and praying; miraculously heals a person's body, soul or spirit.*	3	2	1	0	
U	*Communicates God's message to others when someone speaks in tongues; responds to people who have spoken in a different and unknown language and tells the group what God is saying.*	3	2	1	0	

4

Observation Assessment #1

		Consistently– Definitely True	Most of the Time– Usually True	Some of the Time– Once in a While		Don't Know– Haven't Observed
V	*Speaks God's truth and has it authenticated by an accompanying miracle; communicates the ministry and message of Jesus Christ with demonstrations of power over nature and claims God to be the source of the miracle.*	3	2	1	0	
W	*Speaks in a language I do not understand, and when she or he does, someone speaks out to interpret what they just said; worships God and seems to spontaneously pray using words I have not heard before.*	3	2	1	0	

Here are a few additional questions:

1. Go back over those you marked with a "3" (Consistently/Definitely True) and in the shaded column, indicate your top choice with a 1, second with a 2, and third with a 3. Then write the "letter" of those top three in the space provided to the right.	Top Three Letters 1. _____ 2. _____ 3. _____
2. If you are familiar with Spiritual Gifts, which one(s) have you seen most in this person's life?	1. _____ 2. _____ 3. _____
3. Are there any other observations or insights you have that would help this person better understand what they do best?	Comments

Thank you for taking the time to complete this assessment. Your opinions and observations are valuable to me. I appreciate your help!

5

Spiritual Gifts Discovery

I'd like your opinion!

I am seeking to better understand how God has equipped me to serve others. One part of the process involves getting feedback from a few people who know me reasonably well. Your thoughts about what I do best and the way I relate to others will be very helpful. Please take a few minutes to complete this assessment.

My name is:_____

These are my observations of:

_____

Directions:

1. Please read the descriptions below.

2. Mark each one according to how true it is of the person you are describing.

3. Place your score to each statement in the appropriately numbered box on the answer sheet on pages 2–5. Respond by using the following scale:

SCORE		MEANING
3	=	Consistently/Definitely True
2	=	Most of the Time/Usually True
1	=	Some of the Time/Once in a While
0	=	Don't Know/Haven't Observed

1

IMPORTANT:

- Answer according to what seems to be true of them most of the time ... not what you would like them to be, or think they should be.

- To what degree do these statements reflect their tendencies?

- Return the assessment as soon as you have completed it. Thanks!

Observation Assessment #2

		Consistently– Definitely True	Most of the Time– Usually True	Some of the Time– Once in a While	Don't Know– Haven't Observed
A	Develops strategies or plans to reach identified goals; organizes people, tasks, and events; helps organizations or groups become more efficient; creates order out of organizational chaos.	3	2	1	0
B	Works creatively with wood, cloth, metal, paints, glass, etc.; works with different kinds of tools; makes things for practical uses; designs and builds things; works with his or her hands.	3	2	1	0
C	Communicates with variety and creativity; develops and uses particular artistic skills (art, drama, music, photography, etc.); finds new and fresh ways to communicate ideas to others.	3	2	1	0
D	Strengthens and reassures troubled people; encourages or challenges them; motivates others to grow; supports those who seem to be stuck and need to take action.	3	2	1	0
E	Trusts God to answer prayer and encourages others to do the same; has confidence in God's continuing presence and ability to help, even in difficult times; moves forward in spite of difficulties or opposition.	3	2	1	0

2

Observation Assessment #2

		Consistently— Definitely True	Most of the Time— Usually True	Some of the Time— Once in a While	Don't Know— Haven't Observed	
F	Gives liberally and joyfully to people in financial need; gives generously to projects requiring substantial support; manages his or her money well in order to free more of it for other people and causes.	3	2	1	0	
G	Works behind the scenes to support the work of others; finds small things that need to be done and does them without being asked; helps wherever needed, even with routine or mundane tasks.	3	2	1	0	
H	Meets new people and helps them to feel welcome; entertains guests; opens his or her home to others who need a safe, supportive environment; puts people at ease in unfamiliar surroundings.	3	2	1	0	
I	Continually offers to pray for others; has confidence in the Lord's protection; spends a lot of time praying; is convinced that God moves in direct response to prayer.	3	2	1	0	
J	Takes responsibility for directing groups; motivates and guides others to reach important goals; manages people and resources well; influences others to perform to the best of their abilities.	3	2	1	0	
K	Empathizes with hurting people; patiently and compassionately walks with people through painful experiences; helps those generally regarded as undeserving or beyond help.	3	2	1	0	
L	Pioneers new undertakings (such as a new church or ministry); serves in another country or community; adapts to different cultures and surroundings; demonstrates cultural awareness and sensitivity.	3	2	1	0	
M	Speaks with conviction to bring change in the lives of others; exposes cultural trends, teaching, or events that are morally wrong or harmful; boldly speaks truth even in places where it may be unpopular.	3	2	1	0	

3

Observation Assessment #2

		Consistently– Definitely True	Most of the Time– Usually True	Some of the Time– Once in a While	Don't Know– Haven't Observed	
N	Looks for opportunities to build relationships with unbelievers; communicates openly and effectively about his or her faith; talks about spiritual matters with those who don't believe.	3	2	1	0	
O	Faithfully provides long-term support and nurture for a group of people; provides guidance for the whole person; patiently but firmly nurtures others in their development as believers.	3	2	1	0	
P	Studies, understands, and communicates biblical truth; develops appropriate teaching material and presents it effectively; communicates in ways that motivate others to change.	3	2	1	0	
Q	Distinguishes between truth and error, good and evil; accurately judges character; sees through phoniness and deceit; helps others to see rightness or wrongness in life situations.	3	2	1	0	
R	Carefully studies and researches subjects he or she wants to understand better; shares his or her knowledge and insights with others when asked; sometimes gains information that is not attained by natural observation or means.	3	2	1	0	
S	Sees simple, practical solutions in the midst of conflict or confusion; gives helpful advice to others facing complicated life situations; helps people take practical action to solve real problems.	3	2	1	0	
T	Demonstrates the power of God by bringing restoration to the sick and diseased by laying hands on them and praying; miraculously heals a person's body, soul or spirit.	3	2	1	0	
U	Communicates God's message to others when someone speaks in tongues; responds to people who have spoken in a different and unknown language and tells the group what God is saying.	3	2	1	0	

4

Observation Assessment #2

		Consistently– Definitely True	Most of the Time– Usually True	Some of the Time– Once in a While	Don't Know– Haven't Observed	
V	Speaks God's truth and has it authenticated by an accompanying miracle; communicates the ministry and message of Jesus Christ with demonstrations of power over nature and claims God to be the source of the miracle.	3	2	1	0	
W	Speaks in a language I do not understand, and when she or he does, someone speaks out to interpret what they just said; worships God and seems to spontaneously pray using words I have not heard before.	3	2	1	0	

Here are a few additional questions:

1. Go back over those you marked with a "3" (Consistently/Definitely True) and in the shaded column, indicate your top choice with a 1, second with a 2, and third with a 3. Then write the "letter" of those top three in the space provided to the right.	Top Three Letters 1. _____ 2. _____ 3. _____
2. If you are familiar with Spiritual Gifts, which one(s) have you seen most in this person's life?	1. _____ 2. _____ 3. _____
3. Are there any other observations or insights you have that would help this person better understand what they do best?	Comments

Thank you for taking the time to complete this assessment. Your opinions and observations are valuable to me. I appreciate your help!

5

Spiritual Gifts Discovery

I'd like your opinion!

I am seeking to better understand how God has equipped me to serve others. One part of the process involves getting feedback from a few people who know me reasonably well. Your thoughts about what I do best and the way I relate to others will be very helpful. Please take a few minutes to complete this assessment.

My name is:_____

These are my observations of:

_____

Directions:

1. Please read the descriptions below.

2. Mark each one according to how true it is of the person you are describing.

3. Place your score to each statement in the appropriately numbered box on the answer sheet on pages 2–5. Respond by using the following scale:

SCORE   MEANING
    3 = Consistently/Definitely True
    2 = Most of the Time/Usually True
    1 = Some of the Time/Once in a While
    0 = Don't Know/Haven't Observed

1

IMPORTANT:

- Answer according to what seems to be true of them most of the time ... not what you would like them to be, or think they should be.

- To what degree do these statements reflect their tendencies?

- Return the assessment as soon as you have completed it. Thanks!

Observation Assessment #3

		Consistently– Definitely True	Most of the Time– Usually True	Some of the Time– Once in a While	Don't Know– Haven't Observed
A	Develops strategies or plans to reach identified goals; organizes people, tasks, and events; helps organizations or groups become more efficient; creates order out of organizational chaos.	3	2	1	0
B	Works creatively with wood, cloth, metal, paints, glass, etc.; works with different kinds of tools; makes things for practical uses; designs and builds things; works with his or her hands.	3	2	1	0
C	Communicates with variety and creativity; develops and uses particular artistic skills (art, drama, music, photography, etc.); finds new and fresh ways to communicate ideas to others.	3	2	1	0
D	Strengthens and reassures troubled people; encourages or challenges them; motivates others to grow; supports those who seem to be stuck and need to take action.	3	2	1	0
E	Trusts God to answer prayer and encourages others to do the same; has confidence in God's continuing presence and ability to help, even in difficult times; moves forward in spite of difficulties or opposition.	3	2	1	0

2

Observation Assessment #3

		Consistently– Definitely True	Most of the Time– Usually True	Some of the Time– Once in a While	Don't Know– Haven't Observed
F	Gives liberally and joyfully to people in financial need; gives generously to projects requiring substantial support; manages his or her money well in order to free more of it for other people and causes.	3	2	1	0
G	Works behind the scenes to support the work of others; finds small things that need to be done and does them without being asked; helps wherever needed, even with routine or mundane tasks.	3	2	1	0
H	Meets new people and helps them to feel welcome; entertains guests; opens his or her home to others who need a safe, supportive environment; puts people at ease in unfamiliar surroundings.	3	2	1	0
I	Continually offers to pray for others; has confidence in the Lord's protection; spends a lot of time praying; is convinced that God moves in direct response to prayer.	3	2	1	0
J	Takes responsibility for directing groups; motivates and guides others to reach important goals; manages people and resources well; influences others to perform to the best of their abilities.	3	2	1	0
K	Empathizes with hurting people; patiently and compassionately walks with people through painful experiences; helps those generally regarded as undeserving or beyond help.	3	2	1	0
L	Pioneers new undertakings (such as a new church or ministry); serves in another country or community; adapts to different cultures and surroundings; demonstrates cultural awareness and sensitivity.	3	2	1	0
M	Speaks with conviction to bring change in the lives of others; exposes cultural trends, teaching, or events that are morally wrong or harmful; boldly speaks truth even in places where it may be unpopular.	3	2	1	0

Observation Assessment #3

		Consistently– Definitely True	Most of the Time– Usually True	Some of the Time– Once in a While	Don't Know– Haven't Observed
N	Looks for opportunities to build relationships with unbelievers; communicates openly and effectively about his or her faith; talks about spiritual matters with those who don't believe.	3	2	1	0	
O	Faithfully provides long-term support and nurture for a group of people; provides guidance for the whole person; patiently but firmly nurtures others in their development as believers.	3	2	1	0	
P	Studies, understands, and communicates biblical truth; develops appropriate teaching material and presents it effectively; communicates in ways that motivate others to change.	3	2	1	0	
Q	Distinguishes between truth and error, good and evil; accurately judges character; sees through phoniness and deceit; helps others to see rightness or wrongness in life situations.	3	2	1	0	
R	Carefully studies and researches subjects he or she wants to understand better; shares his or her knowledge and insights with others when asked; sometimes gains information that is not attained by natural observation or means.	3	2	1	0	
S	Sees simple, practical solutions in the midst of conflict or confusion; gives helpful advice to others facing complicated life situations; helps people take practical action to solve real problems.	3	2	1	0	
T	Demonstrates the power of God by bringing restoration to the sick and diseased by laying hands on them and praying; miraculously heals a person's body, soul or spirit.	3	2	1	0	
U	Communicates God's message to others when someone speaks in tongues; responds to people who have spoken in a different and unknown language and tells the group what God is saying.	3	2	1	0	

4

Observation Assessment #3

		Consistently– Definitely True	Most of the Time– Usually True	Some of the Time– Once in a While	Don't Know– Haven't Observed	
V	Speaks God's truth and has it authenticated by an accompanying miracle; communicates the ministry and message of Jesus Christ with demonstrations of power over nature and claims God to be the source of the miracle.	3	2	1	0	
W	Speaks in a language I do not understand, and when she or he does, someone speaks out to interpret what they just said; worships God and seems to spontaneously pray using words I have not heard before.	3	2	1	0	

Here are a few additional questions:

1. Go back over those you marked with a "3" (Consistently/Definitely True) and in the shaded column, indicate your top choice with a 1, second with a 2, and third with a 3. Then write the "letter" of those top three in the space provided to the right.	Top Three Letters 1. _____ 2. _____ 3. _____
2. If you are familiar with Spiritual Gifts, which one(s) have you seen most in this person's life?	1. _____ 2. _____ 3. _____
3. Are there any other observations or insights you have that would help this person better understand what they do best?	Comments

Thank you for taking the time to complete this assessment. Your opinions and observations are valuable to me. I appreciate your help!

5

WILLOW
Willow Creek Association

Willow Creek Association
Vision, Training, Resources for Prevailing Churches

This resource was created to serve you and to help you build a local church that prevails. It is just one of many ministry tools that are part of the Willow Creek Resources® line, published by the Willow Creek Association together with Zondervan.

The Willow Creek Association (WCA) was created in 1992 to serve a rapidly growing number of churches from across the denominational spectrum that are committed to helping unchurched people become fully devoted followers of Christ. Membership in the WCA now numbers over 10,000 Member Churches worldwide from more than ninety denominations.

The Willow Creek Association links like-minded Christian leaders with each other and with strategic vision, training, and resources in order to help them build prevailing churches designed to reach their redemptive potential. Here are some of the ways the WCA does that.

- **Prevailing Church Conference**—an annual two-and-a-half day event, held at Willow Creek Community Church in South Barrington, Illinois, to help pioneering church leaders raise up a volunteer core while discovering new and innovative ways to build prevailing churches that reach unchurched people.

- **Leadership Summit**—a once-a-year, two-and-a-half-day conference to envision and equip Christians with leadership gifts and responsibilities. Presented live at Willow Creek as well as via satellite broadcast to over sixty locations across North America, this event is designed to increase the leadership effectiveness of pastors, ministry staff, volunteer church leaders, and Christians in the marketplace.

- **Ministry-Specific Conferences**—throughout each year the WCA hosts a variety of conferences and training events—both at Willow Creek's main campus and off-site, across the U.S. and around the world—targeting church leaders in ministry-specific areas such as: evangelism, the arts, children, students, small groups, preaching and teaching, spiritual formation, spiritual gifts, raising up resources, etc.

- **Willow Creek Resources®**—to provide churches with trusted and field-tested ministry resources in such areas as leadership, evangelism, spiritual formation, spiritual gifts, small groups, stewardship, student ministry, children's ministry, the use of the arts—drama, media, contemporary music—and more. For additional information about Willow Creek Resources® call the Customer Service Center at 800-570-9812. Outside the U.S. call 847-765-0070.

- *WillowNet*—the WCA's Internet resource service, which provides access to hundreds of transcripts of Willow Creek messages, drama scripts, songs, videos, and multimedia tools. The system allows users to sort through these elements and download them for a fee. Visit us online at www.willowcreek.com.

- *WCA News*—a quarterly publication to inform you of the latest trends, resources, and information on WCA events from around the world.

- *Defining Moments*—a monthly audio journal for church leaders featuring Bill Hybels and other Christian leaders discussing probing issues to help you discover biblical principles and transferable strategies to maximize your church's redemptive potential.

- *The Exchange*—our online classified ads service to assist churches in recruiting key staff for ministry positions.

- **Member Benefits**—includes substantial discounts to WCA training events, a 20 percent discount on all Willow Creek Resources®, access to a Members-Only section on WillowNet, monthly communications, and more. Member Churches also receive special discounts and premier services through WCA's growing number of ministry partners—Select Service Providers.

For specific information about WCA membership, upcoming conferences, and other ministry services contact:

Willow Creek Association
P.O. Box 3188, Barrington, IL 60011-3188
Phone: 847-570-9812
Fax: 847-765-5046
www.willowcreek.com

We want to hear from you. Please send your comments about this book to us in care of zreview@zondervan.com. Thank you.

ZONDERVAN™

GRAND RAPIDS, MICHIGAN 49530 USA

WWW.ZONDERVAN.COM